THE MILES AND THE MARKERS

52 WEEKS OF EXPERIENCES TO IMPROVE YOUR LIVE AND ENHANCE YOUR JOURNEY

GENE GIRDLEY

John,

It has been a pleasure to write a book and work with you. I have learned a lot from you and know it you. Thank you for your support and friendship.

Yours always,

Jim Grubb

Rom 10:9

INTRODUCTION

A great deal was learned while writing The Miles and The Markers. There was self-discovery, and the impact my writing has on others. We don't live our lives on an island or in a vacuum. There is a ripple effect to everything we do. This makes non-fiction, autobiographical material challenging to write. My experience, at least, was painful. It turns out my stories aren't just my stories. Telling a story about fulfilling a personal goal didn't mean it was a dream come true for others.

My intent for writing was to tell stories and experiences to establish credibility. Along the way, I was challenged to use my stories to help others. These are my stories, but they're stories framed in a way that either promote me, help the reader or both. After careful review, this book's focus is not on my personal feelings or emotions, but rather on specific things learned from others in my life.

My hope is this book stimulates decisive action. Personal development begins with a change of mind or a change of heart. Each of us, as individuals, must decide what we will do with our lives. We can choose the destination or just go along for the ride.

My professional business career and most of my adult life have been spent in the automotive industry. Life could have been successful outside the car business, but it's where the journey has taken me. The lessons learned about business and myself may help others learn and avoid some of my pitfalls. I'm still learning, and the "markers" in this book also apply to me. More important is the hope you are inspired, motivated, and moved to take action to improve your life, your leadership skills, and your relationship with others. If you happen to discover a few spiritual things along the way, all the better.

As an ordained minister, it seems strange for me to end up in a business where salespeople are regarded as only more honest than members of Congress. One recent poll has them below politicians at the bottom of the honesty rung of the ladder. My heart has been torn by feelings of a call to ministry or something outside the automotive industry. Not that my calling is to pastor a church, but ministry can happen in many places. Building homes for the needy, providing food for the hungry, and helping care for the sick are all examples of ministry.

People have told me, "what better place to make a difference than in an industry where light is needed?" But is it a lost cause? The individual people certainly are not the problem. Most are exceptional human beings. It's the institutions, the philosophies, and the culture of automotive that makes it challenging. Perhaps my efforts are best suited to helping individuals within the system do the best they can by making the most of every minute of every day.

I am grateful to so many people who have encouraged and continue to support me and provide opportunities for me to learn and grow. As I mentioned already, the auto industry can be both a beacon of light, or a messenger of darkness to consumers, and their people. I've worked for companies whose leaders cared deeply about doing the right thing for their employees and their customers, and for others whose leaders made every decision based on a profit/loss statement or political posturing to save their jobs.

From my days at a local Chevron station to working in dealerships and for automotive OEMs (Original Equipment Manufacturer), these stories are meant to inspire, encourage, and promote change where there are opportunities. Nobody's perfect, and we never arrive! The criticisms related to unnamed individuals, companies, or strategies expressed here are those where reflection is needed for everyone involved, including me. Setbacks in my personal and professional life have caused me to change course several times in my career. A recent private study has me meditating on the idea of "making the crooked straight." Hopefully, others will benefit as a result of my experiences.

Each of us brings our baggage on the journey. Not everyone understands our experiences, and the details are often misinterpreted or taken out of context. One thing is sure: We all need to continue to learn and grow personally and professionally.

Right now, the world is in the middle of the Covid-19 pandemic, and people are scared. Food and other supplies have been hoarded because folks don't know what to do. Many are rebelling against wearing masks, and that complicates things. We, as a human race, are ill-prepared to handle a crisis of this magnitude. We have valued personal "rights", or financial, and corporate success over the fundamentals of humanity, which are otherwise prioritized by a life of faith, love, hope in God, and service to our fellow human family.

Sadly, this lack of focus on caring for others' personal needs has been transferred to the business world and most corporate philosophies. In Simon Sinek's book, *The Infinite Game*, Sinek masterfully explains how the business world has moved from having a just cause to existing to further their stock value and market share. While we have never met, nor do I know anything about Simon Sinek's attitudes toward spiritual things, the principles he espouses are consistent with attitudes of faith and loving others. Read his books.

We've been thrust into a culture war as well. The tragic and brutal death of George Floyd, an African American man, rekindled a problem our society has left unchecked at the hand of a police officer. It's a tragedy that it took nearly a hundred years following the Declaration of Independence, and the death of over half a million men and women who fought in the US Civil War, to put a legal end to slavery. It's even more tragic that after another hundred and forty-five years, all peoples are not treated equally. Racism isn't a phenomenon exclusive to America, though some are pushing that narrative. There is a lot of work to do, and we all should choose to participate.

You'll learn about philosophies that have proven to help me, other individuals and companies, improve relationships with their people, their clients, and their bottom line. If implemented faithfully and consistently, these philosophies promote a positive culture in business, in the home, and society. These include things like the Saturn Values®, The FISH! Philosophy®, and biblical texts. Each of these applies to how we should treat others and how we should lead in our lives, and finally, the leadership of others.

The book is organized into 52 Miles and Markers so you can take one a week if you like. A MARKER is a metaphor for those moments of truth and experience where something significant happens or can happen. It's where and when we can make a difference or where things change. Where and when we can have an impact.

There are statements after each section to encourage you to think and process how these lessons impact you. The Bible says, "Test all things and hold on to that which is good." If it's right for you, use it. If not, move on.

It's my hope everyone reading this understands the power you have to make a difference in this world. While we may fall into the category of mammals, humans are not relegated to behaving solely on instinct. We have the freedom to choose how we will act toward one another. Personal sovereignty is our heritage as imagers of God almighty.

You can choose your attitude, how much time and money to invest in educating yourself, whether or not you'll put the needs of others ahead of your own, and what you will do with the information you read in this book. You can take it or leave it! The emotions or attitudes generated by the words on these pages and how you react to them are your responsibility. Here is wishing you all the best of success in anything and everything you choose to do.

Setting the Tone for The Miles & The Markers

My baseball article published last year on LinkedIn serves to set the tone for my youth and the lessons learned at a young age. It is included here as a tone-setter for the rest of the book.

Baseball Runs in the Family

Dad wanted me to play baseball. The onset of childhood diabetes at age 8 resulted in his early death at 53, and it limited his ability to play most competitive sports. He may have played baseball vicariously through me. While tough at times, I felt pride and joy from the relationship we enjoyed because of baseball.

Uncle Bill almost made it to the big leagues as a member of the original LA Angels in the early 1960s. After dad passed away, I went rummaging through a box of his keepsakes and came across an old LA Times sports page. There in black and white, was a photo of my uncle Billy Girdley sliding into home plate. How cool is that?

From the young age of 7, baseball was significant to me. There was Little League, Senior Babe Ruth Baseball League, high school, college, and semi-pro baseball. I was selected for all-star teams and twice voted all-conference as both a second baseman and a pitcher. I was honored to be part of the 1976 Washington State All-Senior team, and I would eventually pitch against other top players in Seattle's Sick Stadium, the home of the original Seattle Pilots MLB team. What a thrill!

There were beautiful memories. Some I'd like to forget. Each experience contributed to my personal and professional growth. It's a blessing to have played the great game of baseball for so many years.

Pee Wee Reese* I Wasn't

It was a warm, sunny summer afternoon in Norwalk, California, 1967. There stood a towheaded nine-year-old boy in a baggy uniform playing second base. It was the bottom of the third inning, and he desperately needed to pee.

Nobody cares if a kid heads off to the porta-potty to "take a leak" between innings. But in 1967, fathers had high expectations for the sons they were grooming to become major league stars. Sure, I was only nine, but this was serious stuff for my dad! He also happened to be my coach! Had he known I had to pee during the game, a tongue lashing would follow later. "You should have gone before the game," he would have said. Worse yet, he'd pull me out and sit my butt on the bench. This kid wasn't about to say a word. Instead, I held it in and did, "the dance of the ants," for the next two innings.

By the fifth inning, the pressure and burning were too much. My options were to leave the field and face the wrath of dad or cut loose and hope nobody noticed. I chose the latter and peed myself right there at second base in front of everyone. The sizable wet stain that immediately appeared was likely visible by residents of the apartment building next to the ballpark. What an embarrassment!

Aside from the physical relief, and the warm liquid covering my legs and uniform, I don't remember what I thought. I must have mentally checked out. What I do remember is dad calling time out and escorting me from the field to the dugout. As I sat quietly alone on the bench, my dad came over and put his arm around me. "Are you okay," he asked. I cried.

To his credit, dad didn't yell at me or criticize me. My bladder may have gotten the best of me that day, but it didn't hurt my dad's relationship or hinder my future in baseball.

(Pee Wee Reese played shortstop for the Brooklyn and Los Angeles Dodgers from 1940 to 1958 – the year I was born)

Tapped by a Hall of Famer

A few years later, my mom – who happened to be a country-western singer - asked me to go with her to a performance at Tehachapi State Prison in central California. Sharon Leighton and the Country Sunshine were headlining a special event for the inmates, and I was invited to attend. The trip included a 4-hour bus ride each way, and there was no reason to get excited; after all, it was Saturday, with a full morning of Bugs Bunny and Daffy Duck was lined up for my viewing pleasure. Somehow, mom persuaded me that not going would result in untold regret. So off we went.

A few hours later, we found ourselves in the front seat of a Greyhound Bus ready to hit the road. I was bored out of my mind. Then, just before we pulled away from the station, future Hall of Fame pitcher Don Sutton from the Los Angeles Dodgers walked onto the bus. Sutton did motivational speaking and would later become an outstanding broadcaster for the Atlanta Braves.

No one was a bigger Dodger fan than me! Each night during the season, I would fall asleep with an AM radio tucked under my pillow listening through cheap headphones to the immortal Vin Scully calling every moment of every game. I can still hear Scully's call. *"McGraw is at the belt, and here's the pitch. It's a long fly ball to left field. Back goes Jones. Way back. She's gone! A home run for Parker!"*

Before the bus left the station, I felt a tap on my shoulder. Don asked me if I'd like to sit with him for the trip to Tehachapi. "Uh, well. Okay!" Don showed me how, and why, to throw a curveball. Can you imagine the feeling? One of baseball's best had just walked onto my bus and taught me how to pitch. I almost peed myself again!

A Future Champion and a Personal Meltdown

It was my senior year in high school, April of 1976. I was a late bloomer physically, and at seventeen years old, I was only 5'10" tall, and I weighed an unimpressive 155 lbs. I was a right-handed pitcher with an okay fastball and that fantastic curveball I learned to toss on the bus ride years earlier. On an overcast afternoon in the Pacific Northwest, this skinny, brown-haired teenager was about to pitch against a guy who would later become a major league star and win a World Series with the LA Dodgers in 1981. His name was Tom Niedenfeur. At the time, he was about 6'4" and 200 lbs. His fastball reached 90 mph in high school. Big Tom was good!

The bleachers at Redmond High were overflowing with spectators that day. The local press, several college coaches, and a few professional scouts came to watch the matchup. Well, they came to watch Tom. I was just fortunate enough to be his opponent. The first three innings went well as my opponents only got one hit. We were tied 0-0 after three. Then the fourth inning came. Our second baseman made two errors, and Tom's team scored three runs.

We went on to lose the game 3-0 as Tom tossed a no-hitter at us. How we lost is what upset me the most, and I made it known. At 17, I acted like the little kid who wet himself eight years earlier. After the game, everyone heard me stomp my feet; they watched as I threw my glove, and our team felt my anger boiling during the entire bus ride home.

For anyone familiar with baseball, the name Carlos Zambrano is sure to ring a bell. In June of 2010, Zambrano, pitching for the Chicago Cubs, felt as though his teammate Derek Lee should have made more effort to stop a line drive that turned into a double and began a four-run first inning rally for the White Sox. When the inning ended, Carlos went after Lee to such an extent that the Cubs suspended him indefinitely. While my tantrum back in '76 wasn't nearly as bad as Zambrano's, my actions and attitude had on our team, my coach, our fans, and the scouts sitting in the stands was clear: Gene Girdley needed to grow up.

Lesson Learned

The next day one of my coaches saw me about to get into my green Ford F-150 truck and called my name. "Hey Gene," he said with a big smile on his face. "Yeah, Coach?" I replied and turned to face him. Suddenly, I felt two powerful hands gripping the collar of my windbreaker as my heels were lifted slightly off the ground, my back pressed against the front fender of my pickup. My coach's face had turned bright red as his smile transformed into clenched teeth. His pursed lips made it clear he was none too happy. "If you ever disrespect me, your teammates, or this school again," he growled, "I don't care if you're the best pitcher on the planet, you'll never play for this team or me again!" Then he let go of my collar, smiled, and turned away. "See you tomorrow at practice."

Let's be clear, shall we? I was not hurt. Not physically, mentally, or emotionally. It was the coach's way of getting my attention and showing me that he cared. It worked. To this day, I have nothing but the utmost respect and admiration for my coach. He retired as one of the most beloved coaches in school history. He's a kind, gentle soul who gives of his time tirelessly to the local community. In 1976, he did what was needed. He, metaphorically, gave me a good swift kick in my immature pants! I grew up a lot that day. I never again reacted negatively to a teammate, regardless of how they played. We were in this together, and we all needed each other, win or lose. Thanks, Coach!

Professional sports organizations like the NFL now regulate the amount of practice time and physical contact drills in which players can participate. If a coach breaks the rules, the league fines him, and the team forfeits practice time. Individual athletes often employ personal coaches for physical training, goal setting, and psychological/mind training. They've adapted. We should change too.

Final Reflection

During one of those incredible SNL skits from the 70s, Garrett Morris would say, "Baseball been berry, berry good to me!" It has been to me as well. Whether it's parenting, coaching, or selling. Organizations, employees, and customers want and need leaders who can provide a consultative and cooperative approach. People long to be treated with dignity and respect. Dwight D Eisenhower said, "You don't lead by hitting people over the head. That's assault, not leadership." Choose today to adapt and improve your leadership strategies. Your team members and your customers (and maybe even your kids) will love you for it!

ONE

MILE ONE – BEING THERE

MY CAREER in the car business began as a grease monkey at a Chevron gas station in Bellevue, Washington. It was the fall of 1976, and Dave Swap taught me how to do what Marissa Tomei explained to the prosecuting attorney in *My Cousin Vinny*: "Tune-ups, oil changes, brake relining, engine rebuilds, rebuild some tranny's, rear ends..."

Dave was a great shop owner. Besides fixing cars, he taught me how to multitask, treat customers with respect, and up sell to apparent needs on the service drive. In those days, gas stations were full-service. Customers drove over an air hose, and a bell would ring. Before the ring ceased, Dave would leap into action. From under the hood of a 1972 Impala, he would rise, gently set down his half-smoked Camel cigarette, dip out Goop's blob, and rub it into his hands. Out of his pocket came the red shop rag to clean off the grease and back went the dirty rag into his pocket, just as he bent over to ask the once-simple, classic gas station attendant question of: "Fill 'er up?"

If you've worked in the service industry, you're familiar with the term, "feast or famine." It means you're either getting too much or not enough. When it came to customers driving over our air hose, it was always feast or famine. When we had no work in the shop, we'd have virtually no customers wanting gasoline either. But as soon as we found ourselves under the hood for a tune-up, or pulling a wheel to grease the bearings, gas guzzlers would flow in at a constant pace as if they purposely tried to make our day miserable. Pop the hood, "ding." Set the hoist up to raise the car, "ding." And on it went.

After taking the customer's gas order and beginning to pump the petrol, Dave would ask the customer to pop the hood, turn the steering wheel, and turn on the lights. Every customer got their oil checked, and dipstick shown to them. Their fluids were checked and explained, hoses squeezed, belts twisted, tires pressured, tread depth measured, and a quick walk around the vehicle to inspect for burned-out lightbulbs. After the inspection, an offer to repair or replace anything they needed was made. When the bays were full, we'd do service and repairs the old-fashioned way, with a floor jack and an oil drain pan.

Will That Be Cash or Credit?

Dave resisted charging more for credit card purchases until the card companies raised the processing fees beyond what was reasonable. Dave was indeed a customer-focused shop owner. He cared about customers, and he showed me what it meant to "be there" for them, long before the practice was memorialized from the book co-authored by John Christensen called FISH! ®. Dave believed in making a fair profit in exchange for excellent service. He treated me well and allowed me to learn an essential and valuable part of the car business.

Because he didn't have children at the time, Dave treated me like a son. He wanted me to be the guy who could help him build the business beyond a single gas station. When money began to disappear from the cash drawer mysteriously, he was horrified to think it could be me who was taking it. There was only one other potential perpetrator, and he was relatively new.

MILE MARKER
Be there for your customers and others. Prioritize and focus on the most important things for those you're serving.

TWO

MILE TWO - LIVE WITH INTEGRITY

WE WERE TOGETHER when Dave questioned me and my co-worker Gary. Both of us acted shocked at the thought either one might be guilty of petty theft. But it wasn't me, and Gary sounded convincing it wasn't him either. The feeling of being accused is one that causes all kinds of emotions. There's fear, anger, and the hope the whole thing will go away as soon as possible.

This is where personal integrity and abiding faith comes in. While some believe power comes from within, or from the universe, I trust God and in scripture which tells me not to steal or cheat or swindle anyone. Does this sound a bit odd coming from a car guy?

After several days, Dave asked me to work extra hours for a few weeks while he was away helping out his dad. When he returned, he showed me the video tape of Gary taking the money out of the cash drawer. I'm not sure if it was me or Dave who was happier it wasn't me who had been taking twenty-dollar bills from the cash register. It was a relief to me, but a horrible outcome for Gary. He was a nice kid who found himself in a difficult situation personally. He also had less than stellar influences in his life at the time without having a dad at home. To his credit, Dave didn't turn him in to the police. He simply asked Gary to return the money he'd taken after he was let go. He was more than happy to oblige, and he certainly learned a lesson in grace.

Dave taught me many valuable lessons including a positive work ethic, honesty and integrity in business, and how to sell, all while treating customers and employees with dignity and respect. He showed me how to switch focus and what to prioritize. While there were promise times to keep with respect to repairs, nothing was more important than being there for a customer who was right in front of you. Which leads to another marker.

MILE MARKER

Your level of integrity shouldn't change when circumstances change. Stand for what is right regardless of outside pressures or influences.

THREE

MILE THREE – USE TECHNOLOGY WISELY

TECHNOLOGY IS awesome when used correctly. A simple story may help with this lesson. Years ago, a colleague asked me to observe a training pilot for a tablet tool being used on the service drive. The dealership was participating in the project for Honda as an early adopter. Tablets were pretty new to both dealerships and consumers twenty years ago.

The good part about using the tablet was it allowed the service advisor to perform the entire write up and meet with the customer at their vehicle. This made the vehicle walk-around and explanation of services a much more simple and convenient way to manage the customer experience. But then a key feature of the tablet was activated, and the entire experience went from great to horrible.

You see this tablet had an inbound call feature built in to allow the advisor to see the exact customer who was calling them, including the repair order number for quick access to pulling up the file. The problem occurred when the trainer told the advisor to immediately leave the customer they were with and take the call. This is equivalent to cursing and goes against every customer experience standard there is.

Never leave the customer who is right in front of you. Be there, giving them your full consideration.

There's currently a debate over the use of kiosks and other technology on the service drive and for customer interaction. Like the tablet in our story, kiosks have many benefits. But if both consumers and advisors aren't trained on how to use them and what the specific limitations are, the system will fail. Being there for your customers is still better when done by human-to-human interaction. The argument from the technology camp is that people don't do their jobs and technology does the job consistently and the same way every time with every customer. To me, this is a training and leadership issue, regardless of the technical solutions available.

Later in the book there's a problem with technology that comes up in my experience managing the service department at Saab. Here's an important question: How many people know how to get the job done when technology fails? Can they do things using paper and pen? Can they calculate and do simple math? What are the backup plans and resources?

This is in no way an indictment against technology. Technology is awesome and useful. But many viciously oppose the newest technology in customer interactions. One example comes from the world of automotive. In one camp we have the traditionalists who believes the needs of the customer should be discovered by a human advisor, face-to-face. In the other camp are those who promote kiosks which allow the customers to do it themselves. How might we approach advancements or changes to culture?

A story from the Bible may provide wisdom for those who argue against the use of new technology like kiosks or apps. In Acts 5:34, a dispute arises among the religious leaders of the day regarding what action to take against the new Christian movement known at the time as, "The Way." A wise pharisee named Gamaliel told the group, "In the present case I advise you: Leave these men alone! Let them go! For if their purpose or activity is of human origin, it will fail. But if it is from God, you will not be able to stop these men; you will only find yourselves fighting against God."

If customers find technology like kiosks or apps to be better for them than traditional methods, nothing we can do will stop the use of that technology. But if customers' needs aren't met, or dealerships don't become more profitable or efficient as a result, the new tech will end up in a storage closet much like dealership tablets have on many service drives. So, don't sweat it. Let the kiosk companies and app companies give it their best. If customers love it, why fight against the customer? After all, aren't we doing what we do for the customer?

MILE MARKER

Put processes in place for every aspect of the customer experience regardless of whether there is technology involved. People are the most important aspect of both your processes, and the technology you choose.

FOUR

MILE FOUR – DO THE RIGHT THING

BEING there for people is how Jesus lived. We can learn a great deal about how we should live and behave in business from the way Jesus modeled life. In his letter to the church at Philippi, the apostle Paul explained, "Have this mind among yourselves, which is yours in Christ Jesus, who, though he was in the form of God, did not count equality with God a thing to be grasped, but emptied himself, by taking the form of a servant..." (Phil 2:5-7 ESV).

Dave Swap taught me some 45 years ago the types of behaviors service departments should be doing today. With modern innovations and technology, the customer experience and ability for dealerships to deliver great service and make money should be a no brainer. Sadly, the only no brainer seen today is the resistance of manufactures, dealers, and dealership managers (and even some technicians) to meet the customers where they are and deliver to them what they want. Great service at a reasonable price.

Instead, their egos are standing in the way resulting in dealerships losing most of their service business to independent shops. They've followed in the footsteps of Kodak who had the ability to move to digital before anyone else, but they didn't want to lose their film, paper, and processing sales by advancing technology. Independent service centers today take over 80% share of the maintenance and repair business. Convenience and ease of transaction are two key elements associated with lost dealership business. Reputation is another.

For decades dealerships gouged customers with high prices, while allowing technicians to short-cut warranty repair processes. Many technicians are offended that the manufacturer isn't paying them enough for taking care of their customers, so many don't take the time to fix the vehicle right the first time. This is an understandable reaction. I recently spoke to a technician who is retiring in part because he does fix the vehicles right, but he's not being paid fairly for his time.

Most manufacturers aren't willing to pay a fair price for diagnosing certain problems that require more time. It's similar to what we see happening today in health care, where insurance companies pay physicians a small percentage of the contracted charges, affording doctors only a small amount of time (5 to 15 minutes) in order to diagnose a problem. By limiting the amount of time doctors have to diagnose a problem, the end result is obvious: Less than stellar patient care.

Due in part to Covid-19, new vehicle sales started shrinking, but there has been a bit of a comeback. The future of new vehicle sales as a key profit center is unknown. Manufactures and dealerships are being forced to reconsider the importance of their service departments.

Success in fixed operations is the only hope many will have if they're going to survive. Service directors, trainers, and managers are taking the lead on their own to form mastermind groups and to reintroduce traditional, yet still successful strategies of doing business. These are the proven strategies Dave Swap taught me four decades ago.

Another story from my retail days illustrates the contrast between the right way and the wrong way. Years ago, a lady and her daughter drove past our dealership. She saw a bright yellow coupe on our lot, and she had to have it. Considering it was our last one, we wrote up the contract and performed a blind appraisal on her trade-in. Since her existing vehicle was a Toyota that had five trim lines, we informed her that the appraised value was based on her accurate description, but that it could change one way or another. She agreed.

The next day she brought in her trade and we appraised it. She thought her model was two full trims lower than it was. In other words, her car was worth more money.

When telling this story to managers in training, I would ask them how they would handle the extra gross found in the trade. Over half said to take it all. Twenty-five percent said to split the difference so she would feel good about it. Only one quarter of the managers said she deserved all the money. We gave her all the money.

As a result, the customer told our local newspaper about how we treated her and no fewer than twenty customers came in over the next few weeks with newspaper in hand. They wanted to do business with an honest, fair dealership for a change.

The concern today is manufacturers who continue to push wholesale on dealers so hard they both destroy their network of dealerships and destroy the lives of their field people. These are their internal customers.

When are manufacturers going to accept the fact our global production capabilities are at least twice that of consumer demand? And with subscription models becoming a favorable alternative, our industry can't continue with a status quo mentality. It's time to change our approach or watch disruptors completely takeover the automotive business world.

From a biblical perspective, people in power shouldn't use their power or authority against people without it. Jesus warned against following those with power, saying, "They tie up heavy loads that are hard to carry and put them on people's shoulders, but they themselves aren't willing to lift a finger to move them...they love places of honor at banquets...and greetings in the marketplace..." While this scripture spoke of the religious leaders of the day, the description sounds like the behavior of some manufacturers, lenders, car dealers and managers who have given our industry a bad name.

MILE MARKER

Do the right thing for your people (internal customers) and your retail guests (external customers) regardless of the short-term financial impact. Doing the right thing results in long-term success, as well as both employee and customer retention.

FIVE

MILE FIVE – BE OPEN TO NEW IDEAS

ABOUT 18 MONTHS after my work began with Dave Swap, an opportunity arose to learn from another mechanic. He served in Honduras as a missionary six months out of the year. By coincidence, his name was Dave too. It's funny, but many of the people who have impacted my life have been named David. My best friend as a boy was named David. The biblical King David is someone close to my heart. We gave one of our sons the middle name David. And it makes sense any man whose name means "beloved" would be a servant of others.

While not on the mission field, Dave and his wife ran quite a unique repair business. He serviced people's cars and trucks wherever they happened to be: At work, at school, or home. He drove a Willys Jeep Wagon, which doubled as his shop.

After connecting at church one Sunday, Dave told me

his business had so much work that he was scheduling customers two to three weeks out, just for oil changes. And there was the issue of when he was away on a mission. Dave needed to be there to support the customers needing service work. He assured me my technical skills were more than adequate, so Gene's Auto-Doc was born. It provided maintenance services and minor repairs out of my bright yellow Ford Pinto station wagon, complete with faux woodgrain side panels.

Thirty years later, my BDC (Business Development Center) was responsible for scheduling mobile service vans for four Southern California dealerships. Mobil service was uncommon in the 1990s, and it hasn't been something most dealerships wanted to do until Covid-19 forced their hand. Now more dealerships are doing mobile service and providing customers with exceptional experiences away from the retail establishment.

Telling the story of Gene's Auto-Doc and my background as a mechanic, people assume I love cars. As a young boy, there were slot cars and the soapbox derby event. My dad was into having hot rods and speed boats, so it stands to reason his love for vehicles and engines would transfer to me. As a teenager, my best friend and I collected Hot Wheels, and we would set up a track and race them every weekend.

But I'm not in love with the technical aspect of cars. Don't ask me to look at a car and name the year, make, and model like so many who love cars. When people introduce me as a real car guy, they indicate my knowledge and understanding of the business and process side of the automotive industry. After ten years with Mitsubishi, I'm pretty knowledgeable about their product. But had I been a "car guy," I would likely have stayed a mechanic.

MILE MARKER
Listen to new ideas. Be open to looking at new opportunities for your clients and for ways to grow personally and professionally.

SIX

MILE SIX – SLOW DOWN TO SPEED UP

RUNNING an auto repair company wasn't an easy gig. There was a lot of running to the parts store and working in the rain, but the ability to choose my schedule and have some level of flexibility was positive. Learning the art of diagnosing and analyzing was the highlight of my time working with Dave. He was a genius at fixing cars, and he shared some of his knowledge with me. He was especially good with electrical problems and analysis. The art of diagnosing has been lost on many. Dave taught me to take my time, a concept you can apply to most things in life called "slow down to speed up."

Once while managing the service department at Saab of Orange County, I took a call from a customer who had an intermittent issue with her air-conditioning. I asked the right questions and learned that the problem occurred after the vehicle was driven for at least 15 minutes. When the car arrived, I wrote the repair order with specific details explaining what caused the failure to occur. But the technician was busy, and within five minutes of dispatching the job, he plopped the ticket back on my desk with NPF (No Problem Found) stamped on the front. He hadn't even driven the car.

Because he was swamped (no excuse for a poor diagnosis), I jumped in the car and hopped on the freeway. Sure enough, the AC quit after about 15 minutes. I also noticed as soon as it failed, the temperature gauge stopped working. That helped the technician diagnose the problem, and the fix was rather simple. But this type of thing happens all the time. In cases where the technician feels rushed, the vehicle is often returned to the customer without being fixed. The result is more time for everyone, poor customer experiences and reviews, and a loss of revenue.

Today's vehicles are more complicated than they used to be, but the complications have been somewhat reduced by software and technology. This advancement is both a blessing and a curse when it comes to vehicle repairs. The benefit is a technician can simply plug in a scan tool and read an error code to isolate the area of the problem. Most of us can buy a simplified version of a tool like this on the internet.

A failed part or wire can create error codes after being chewed on by a mouse. It could be a loose connection. The code identifying the problem's area doesn't tell the technician the actual cause of the problem. Determining the real cause requires diagnosis. Slow down, to speed up!

Slowing down to speed up isn't just about fixing things. It applies to many areas of life. Planning a trip is one example; most people don't just jump in a car and go on vacation. Why should you operate your business or work without slowing down and planning?

MILE MARKER

Focus on quality, not just quantity. Take the time to ensure you're doing the job right the first time. Taking more time upfront may seem to take longer, but you're saving time and money in the end.

SEVEN

MILE SEVEN – PAY ATTENTION TO LIFE'S CLUES

AS A YOUNG MAN, faith wasn't something to be taken seriously. My profession of faith was based on semi-regular church attendance. That's all. Attending church doesn't make you a Christian any more than working in a garage makes you a mechanic. You may have the title or certification, and you may still be part of the team, but you need to learn a lot more before you can say you know your stuff. Expertise applies to every area of life. The emphasis on college degrees is valuable for professions where life and death, or significant sciences or engineering are involved. Most other things can be learned on y]

During the past forty years, my studies have helped me come to understand how to read and apply the Bible. It's packed with wisdom and practical life skills. The scriptures say the Word of God is living and active, and the Spirit of God works inside us to expose our imperfections and refine our lives. The eventual outcome is intended to be a life more closely resembling Christ Himself. Why would anyone argue against being more Christlike? It doesn't matter what we do in life, but it does matter who we become. "He (Christ) who began a good work in you will complete it...", says the scriptures.

We often fail to grasp how our lives are unfolding as we're living them. It's the old, "can't see the forest for the trees," analogy. For me, having the mindset of an entrepreneur wasn't something that entered my mind. But forty years later, being an entrepreneur is where I find myself. In retrospect, it is likely why boredom set in so quickly after just a few years at a particular job.

My experience may help save you a lot of grief and a lot of wasted time. When I look back, it's clear now my calling has been to lead. But circumstances and the influence of others caused me to question that. You would rarely find me doing something on my own. Take my fifth-grade talent show. I planned to sing a song by Glenn Campbell called Wichita Lineman. He sang it as a solo, and I practiced singing it by myself. But the fear of failure made me decide not to do it alone, and another boy needed an act in the show. Since neither one of us was very confident, the performance bombed.

To this day, my default position is to look for someone else to do it with me. There's nothing wrong with involving others. It's vital to success. But if you're called to lead, or if your purpose is to be an entrepreneur, then there are decisions, choices, and actions you must take on your own. For me, it's also with God's help and guidance. The sooner you find your purpose, the easier it will be to understand why you do what you do. It will help others understand you as well. You may be in the role of a leader, whether you own your own business or not. If you like being the boss or a leader, it's essential to embrace it now. Once you do, you'll at least understand why they say, "It's lonely at the top!"

MILE MARKER

Examine who you are, how you think, and what drives you. Know and understand your gifts, skills, talents, and passions. Then you will be able to set the tone for a successful future.

EIGHT

MILE EIGHT – BELIEVING MEANS DOING

REGARDLESS OF YOUR FAITH, your values, or the philosophies, you should understand actions matter. There was a debate among the writers of the books I read when my sales career began. Many who were motivational speakers would be questioned by business philosophers and process gurus and vice versa. On the surface, there seems to be a disconnect, but both are important. What you do with the information you receive is the key to success.

Jim Rohn once said, "Motivation alone is not enough. If you have an idiot and you motivate him, now you have a motivated idiot."

By contrast, Zig Ziglar said, "You don't have to be great to start, but you have to start to be great. People often say that motivation doesn't last. Well, neither does bathing – that's why we recommend it daily."

Whenever we promote a value, a philosophy, a religious principle, or any other practice, it is incumbent upon us to live it. The first of Saturn's five values is commitment to customer enthusiasm. This principle was the basis for our consistently high survey scores. We were so committed to the values, we carried them on cards in our pockets for quick reference.

The cards came in handy after we sold a used vehicle to an E-1 serviceman stationed at Camp Pendleton. The car was listed, "as is," on the buyer's guide, and he could ill afford a service contract. The following Saturday, he called me to let me know his car wouldn't start. We had it towed, and we determined a replacement battery was needed. Legally we had no obligation to replace it, but my approach was to have the service department do it anyway.

When my sales manager saw the "we owe" bill, she said, "I'm not paying for that! The sale was 'as is,' and we have no obligation to pay for it!" My response was simple: I placed the values card was on the table and pointed to, "commitment to customer enthusiasm". "You're right," my manager said, and she signed the paper.

Faith works the same way. James says, "Faith without works is dead." That in no way mitigates God's grace, but if we don't act on our faith, then what's the use? I've done plenty of street testimonials, singing about Jesus in public, and serving on the mission field in other countries and the inner cities. I'm not boasting. It's just a story to illustrate another mile marker in my life.

MILE MARKER

Be a person of action. Follow through on your commitments and live your stated values. No one will trust or believe you if you don't act on what you say you think.

NINE

MILE NINE – LEARN FROM EVERY LEADER

MY FIRST PASTOR, Wayne Taylor, drove a school bus part-time and began his ministry hosting a home group of believers who listened to Chuck Smith cassette tapes. Wayne played guitar and had a passion for the Bible nobody had shown me before. Being one of Wayne's disciples and learning biblical fundamentals from him was great. More importantly, learning what it meant to love Jesus from watching Wayne's life was even better.

When not reading the Bible or working, I learned to play guitar, and I participated in street witnessing with the group from Calvary Fellowship in Seattle. To learn new music, I picked up a little worship songbook illustrated by Greg Laurie called "Rejoice in Jesus Always." A copy is still in my library, and Greg has gone on to lead one of the largest evangelical ministries in the world, called Harvest Crusades.

It wasn't long before leading worship at the college bible

study on Wednesday evenings at Bellevue Community College was a weekly event for me. Three years later, my ministry would be to lead the congregation on Sunday mornings for Pastor Lee Bennet's Calvary Northshore in Bothell, Washington. Lee brought elements of psychology and understanding human behavior into his teaching.

I would later be ordained and serve as junior high director, youth pastor, and pastor of lay ministries at Ocean Hills Community Church in San Juan Capistrano, California. During that time, my travels took me to Israel to learn about the Bible in the place where it all happened. Several pastors taught me leadership skills, including Jim Glynn, Paul Spitz, Homer Waisner, and Ridge Burns. Working with Ridge allowed my wife and I to do ministry in places where most people would choose not to serve—the ghettos and slums of the inner cities and impoverished areas of Mexico.

Along the way, we developed some pretty cool things in ministry. One of our ideas was published in a youth ministry magazine with the cover feature noting our "CIA" (Christians In Action) idea. The goal was to get our "agents" to do regular study, acts of kindness, and other services similar to the scouts, except this was based on biblical principles of witnessing and discipleship. Students earned a promotion to different levels, with the ultimate achievement being the rank of "spy." We were later contacted by a ministry in Colorado wanting to develop this further since they had created the MAFIA (Mothers and Fathers Interested in Adolescence).

Another influential minister was author and Christian leader Jim Burns. According to his current bio, he is "the president of HomeWord. He speaks to thousands of people around the world each year. He has close to 2 million resources in print in 20 languages." At the time, Jim taught youth ministers how to reach kids better. One of the first things Jim said was, "We were never their age," meaning life is different in ways we can't fully comprehend. This idea is truer today as a global culture and technology complicates generational and social changes. Jim taught us another phrase that is important to developing content: "The essence of creativity is the ability to copy."

MILE MARKER

Look for strengths in others and seek to follow their example. Become a lifelong learner and impart what you've learned to others.

TEN

MILE TEN – BE EFFICIENT AND BE POSITIVE

WHILE SERVING IN MINISTRY, the need to do side work in construction, automotive, and appliance repair remained. Youth work doesn't pay well in most cases. During that time, one of my favorite leaders was Steve Larson. Steve ran a home building company that began with framing houses. Steve taught me many things about construction that transfer to other aspects of life and work. One important thing he taught me was efficiency and continuous improvement. Steve taught me never to walk anywhere without carrying something that needed to go where I was going.

Efficiency is required in just about every enterprise, be it sports, work, or home. In the car business, it means proper use of time for yourself, your team, and your customers. Developing and consistently following appropriate processes help. As a leader, modeling these behaviors and measuring compliance is an essential aspect of superior management skills.

Steve also modeled a behavior we teach in FISH! ® called "Choose Your Attitude." There were times when the weather was horrible, or in the summer, we'd have to deal with yellow jacket swarms, and Steve always found a way to choose to be positive. He also looked for ways to get better.

On one particular day, we were framing the second floor of a two-story saltbox-style home while Steve was "cutting in" the stairs. It turned out the architect had drawn a significant support beam right through the stairwell, so anyone walking up the stairs was hit squarely in the face by a 6x12. Of course, the architect said we did something wrong until he came out to the job site and realized his mistake. In most cases, the crew would have been sent home without pay until they figured out what to do. Steve had us lock things up, took us to lunch, and paid us to play a skeet shooting game at the local pub until later that afternoon when the architect showed up. He never got emotional about anything.

Practicing each of your daily routines with a positive growth mindset is vital to your continued success. Having the proper mindset requires you to choose the appropriate attitude for the proper situation. Where you end up as a leader and your team ends up collectively and individually, depends on your attitude and your approach toward continuous improvement.

MILE MARKER

Choose to have the appropriate attitude. Look for ways to be efficient and always seek to continuously improve.

ELEVEN

MILE ELEVEN – SALES IS AN HONORABLE PROFESSION

IN EARLY 1995, while eating breakfast at Mollies Café, my eyes came across an advertisement in the local newspaper for the job of sales consultant for Saturn of San Juan Capistrano in California. My current contract work had been repairing appliances but laying on my back and getting filthy wasn't my favorite thing to do every day.

From my experience with a car salesman and my ministry background, one would never have considered me to be someone who would sell cars. Prior to selling cars, my wife and had an experience involving a negotiation ending with the sales manager slamming a book down and screaming at us to, "Take the fu**ing car!" And who can forget Cal Worthington and his dog spot, or Ralph Williams and his foul-mouthed straight to the point comments you can still find on YouTube? But the advertisement said, "Traditional car salesman need not apply!" I showed up with a resume in hand the next day.

The process my career would take later would be to learn, and teach, the story behind Saturn Corporation and how different it indeed was. Their slogan was, "A Different Kind of Company, A Different Kind of Car!" The story goes that my dealer principal, John Campbell, had found his way to Saturn through a conversation with Carl Sewell. Carl wrote the book *Customers for Life*. John was already selling cars with a no-hassle, no-haggle approach at his existing dealerships, so when Carl mentioned Saturn's customer strategy, it seemed like a perfect fit for him.

My understanding is, John's Saturn of Orange County was the first market area in the country to be signed up as a new Saturn franchise. The values Saturn developed fit me like a glove. They included things like focusing on customer enthusiasm, teamwork, and continuous improvement. It was on this foundation that my career in sales is built. It was also based on an approach toward customer education and information. Being a former teacher and minister made this a smooth transition. I've never really seen myself as a salesperson. I've always been an educator.

Two quotes from Zig Ziglar regarding sales made all the difference for me in my career. The first is, "You can get everything you want in life, as long as you help enough other people get what they want." The second is, "Don't try to change someone's mind. Help them make a new decision based on new information." My career has skyrocketed partly because of my sales success, and in part because of my past as an educator and minister.

MILE MARKER
Understand the qualities of a sales professional such as

honesty and integrity. Provide value in your products and services and make sure they meet your clients' wants and needs.

TWELVE

MILE TWELVE - VALUES MATTER

MY CAREER in car sales began in April of 1995. I've been successful in part due to the mission, values, and philosophy of the dealer and the brand he represented: Saturn. Had it not been a company whose motto included being different, it's doubtful my life would have ended up the way it has. But you never know. God works in mysterious ways.

On my first day, it was clear something was different. This place was fun. People were laughing and clapping, and the customers were smiling—what a refreshing environment. There were five of us in training on the first day. Dennis Joy, our general sales manager, introduced us by saying, "We're pretty laid back here. Let's give each other a big hug." That wasn't an issue for me because we did that a lot at church. The rest of the group appeared to be okay with it too, but in today's world of "#metoo" and Covid-19, that experience would not have occurred, and it may not ever again.

The training was similar to ministry training. The values were in line with caring for people and one another on the team. Continuous improvement was a value that was embraced by the Christian faith. Everything about the Saturn mission, philosophy, and values aligned perfectly with my faith and life as a believer in Jesus. I was home. My experience then, also aligns now, with the FISH! ® Philosophies of "Make Their Day" and "Play!"

Every new and used car delivery was an event. The cleaned and readied vehicle would be placed in a delivery module because customers enjoyed driving their new car off the showroom floor. Each team member would be notified via a pager that a vehicle delivery was about to take place. We would immediately begin to clap, and all of us would converge on the customer and the vehicle. The sales consultant would introduce the customer to the team, and we would all cheer for the customer. They loved it.

I once had a retired Ford dealer visit my store to learn what was going on. He'd heard about Saturn. He told me under no circumstance would he ever pay full price for a car. And he never bought one from us. But he did love the celebration so much he referred three people to me, and he came to watch the delivery of every one of them. He loved to watch us play!

Another time a team member called me at home and asked me to meet him at a restaurant to do a surprise delivery. "Of course," was my reply. In another instance, we delivered a car to a rabbi on the Sabbath. He had to leave before completing the paperwork because the sun was setting. These stories go on and on about how we lived Saturn's mission, values, and philosophy.

MILE MARKER

Have a clear vision, mission, philosophy, and values.

Everyone on your team should understand them, live them, and effectively articulate them to one another and your clients.

THIRTEEN

MILE THIRTEEN – LEARN ALL YOU CAN

DURING THE ORIENTATION PROCESS, Dennis, and my other manager Becky, helped me lay a solid foundation for sales success. The first thing he did was introduce me to authors like Jim Rohn, Zig Ziglar, Brian Tracy, and Jim Cathcart. These gentlemen introduced me to other inspirational authors they learned from like Napoleon Hill, George S. Clason, Dale Carnegie, and many more. My lifelong love affair with inspirational books began, and I've never looked back.

    I recently interviewed a great leader with whom most of you should be familiar: Brian Tracy. I met Brian in 2004, and I've followed his work and his writings for years. I thought it might be fun to put out a question to my network, asking if anyone would like me to pose a question to Brian. One of my connections responded with, "What is your biggest lesson from the downtime during Covid-19?" He then added, "Gene, can I ask you the same question?"

Many things have happened as a result of Covid–19 that impacted my life and business. For example, I would not have done, nor would I be doing, virtual events with Ted Ings' Fixed Ops Roundtable®. These virtual events opened up a number of opportunities for me, including the chance to interview comedian and entertainer Jay Leno.

Instead, my time would have been spent on the road for Mitsubishi in their dealerships. As I reflected on this, one thing came to mind that both prepared me for the pandemic and helped me through it.

ALWAYS BE LEARNING NEW SKILLS!

I say that because I've had that philosophy since I was a young man, and it's acted as a huge savings account when Covid–19 hit us. I quickly pivoted from a live training role to skills I had developed years ago, including video production, scripting and editing, on-camera hosting, course development, and writing. Besides occasional content writing and webinars, I hadn't done much of that for the past ten years. But now, those skills are in high demand when in-dealership training is non-existent."

With respect to Brian's answer, you'll have to listen to The Fixed Ops Roundtable® podcast to get the full details. But he did remind our listeners of one important learning based on his years of management and leadership experience. Continue to work hard and know this too shall pass.

MILE MARKER

Always be learning. This creates a "skills and knowledge" savings account you can tap into when needed. Always be hungry for more and new information.

FOURTEEN

MILE FOURTEEN – FOLLOW UP & FOLLOW THROUGH = SUCCESS

THE SECOND THING Dennis did was explain to me how he had become successful in sales. He told me he would give me the secret to becoming the number one sales consultant in the company. Here is the conversation:

"You simply need to do one thing consistently."

"What is it?"

"Follow up!"

"Did you give the same speech to everyone else on the team?"

"Yes!"

"Then why do you think I'll be number one if you've told the same story to everyone else?"

"Because I think you'll do it!"

He was right.

At the end of my first full year in sales, my numbers led all other salespeople in total gross profit, and my sales volume was second by one unit to the top salesperson among four retail facilities. My path in automotive was already determined to be training other people to be successful in the car business, and specifically, as a trainer for Saturn Corporation. In my first full year with Campbell Automotive's Saturn brand, my success was reaching the ultimate personal goal of every one of John Campbell's employees, which was to achieve acceptance into the elite President's Club.

To work in automotive sales traditionally requires long hours. Sometimes 6 to 7 days a week working 30 days or more without a day off isn't unheard of for new salespeople. It doesn't mean the company requires it. It just means commissioned sales is a profession that is more like owning your own business than it is a 9-to-5 job. You need to follow through on your commitments and do what it takes to meet your goals.

People who don't look at sales as their own business are rarely successful. Being an entrepreneur, it's not a surprise I took to it as a duck takes to water. Any new business requires hard work and long hours. People may tell you otherwise, and you may be tempted to jump at a new business idea or concept that suggests it is easy to start a business and make a lot of money. Companies aren't that difficult to start, but they are challenging to build into a success and maintain that success.

MILE MARKER

Follow up with every customer regularly and follow through on every promise. Establish long term relationships based on the things that are important to your customers, not what is important to you.

FIFTEEN

MILE FIFTEEN – TRAINING SHOULD BE PRIORITIZED AND SCHEDULED

I RECENTLY COMPLETED a course called *The Neuroscience of Learning*. I was encouraged because many of the strategies I've used in my work were reinforced. For example, the part of your brain that helps you remember things can only work on one thing for a maximum of twenty minutes. That's why educators should switch things up every fifteen minutes or so. I practice that in my courses, both live and online.

Training was essential to the Campbell Automotive Group. John paid employees fifty dollars a day to attend training, plus food and gas (that was a reasonable amount in 1995). It may not sound like much, but a lot of companies wouldn't pay a thing. Trying to get anyone to attend offsite training today is like pulling teeth, and yet it's vital to learning that people be afforded an environment without distractions. Because, according to recent studies, "multitasking" is a myth. The brain can't truly focus on more than one thing at a time and retain the information.

While skills are lacking more than ever, many corporations are training less and less, even though there should be more available time than ever before. When training is offered, it's been trimmed down to nothing more than a motivational session or a discussion about new technology. Gone are the three-day sales intensive workshops. In the automotive world, live training it's typically three hours maximum, delivered at a hotel, or a day or two in a dealership where salespeople are continually being pulled out of class to take customers. As a result, most training is relegated to web-based self-study courses the manufacturers require for certification. In many cases, managers pay other people to take the exams for their team. It's pretty sad.

This new approach to training is problematic. As I discovered in *The Neuroscience of Learning*, retention requires a process that takes time. Retrieval (unlike repetition) is a process that includes proper sleep, then a revisiting of the information in several sessions. Today there is no time and no budget for training. It's a shame too, because most people begin their careers with little if any applicable knowledge or skills.

When my career in sales began, all customer contact employees had off-site training once a quarter. It was a three-hour drive on a Monday at 5 a.m. for me to get to the GM training center. Managers attended as well, so they could reinforce the training throughout the weeks and months that followed. We attended specialized training for a week in Springhill, Tennessee, for which our dealership paid. Other than one-to-one coaching or new hire orientation, all training took place away from the dealership in those days.

MILE MARKER

Be dedicated to quality, ongoing training for your team. Provide them with the necessary time, free from other distractions. Provide them with skills, tools, and resources to help them become the best they can be, even if that means they leave your company to fulfill their dreams.

Note: Since I began writing this book, almost all training has been done virtually due to the pandemic, and we're just starting to return to live training at dealerships. What interests me is this: While virtual training is significantly less money, car dealerships and manufacturers have, in many cases, cut their entire training budgets unless they have a new product launch planned. They say they've done this because sales have dried up and their profits are down. The analogy I use is the farmer (who just had a bad crop) telling God that if he only brings a miracle harvest, he'll plant seeds next year. Does that make sense? I'm not sure who sold management that bill of goods.

SIXTEEN

MILE SIXTEEN – TRAINING SHOULD BE FUN AND ENGAGING

HAVING BEEN A TEACHER, youth pastor, and a preacher, being creative and comfortable in front of a group hasn't been an issue. During one of my world history lessons on the expansion of Europe, I had my junior high students create a giant map of the continent in the middle of the room. We divided each of the areas into a game of risk, and we weighted the "armies" of each tribe (Goths and Visigoths) to ensure the expansion would unfold as it did historically. We had a teaching intern from UC San Diego at the time, and she was blown away at how the kids learned.

One of my first training classes required in automotive sales was on certified used cars. Given my learning attitude is it should be interactive and fun, my tolerance for anyone who simply stood in front of a projector and read bullet points off a slide was low. After returning from the class, my manager Dennis asked me how it went. My response was,

"The trainer sucked!" It would have gone better if they'd given me the materials the day before and let me do it. Two months later, I went to Springhill, Tennessee, to attend two other classes, *Saturn Cultures and Values* and *The Saturn Consultative Sales Process*. My view of corporate culture and training forever changed.

The ride on the bus from Nashville to the factory was fun. There were some great stories about the area, and everyone was excited to participate. Many had been waiting a year to attend, as several dealers wanted to be sure they weren't going to lose out on their investment by sending someone who might quit after just a few months. But they were there now, and all of us spilled enthusiasm on each other as if we were little kids. We'd heard nothing but magical stories about visiting the Saturn factory at Springhill

Later in the afternoon we loaded a bus and toured the factory, learning about the unique ways Saturn showed respect for the environment, the local neighbors, and the customers who visited the factory in an event called "The Saturn Homecoming," which drew over 100,000 owners. There were more stories about the Antebellum mansions on the property as we drove to a ropes course and to the events hall called "Spider Holler."

Spider Holler is where we participated in a blind sherpa walk, a trust fall, and other team building activities designed to help us learn how much we needed one another. It felt like a youth camp. By the end of the day, my mind was set that this was the company for me. Becoming a facilitator for Saturn's Retail Training Team was now at the top of my bucket list.

A SIDE STREET CALLED DIVERSITY

Today my contract work includes directing and

producing Ted Ing's Fixed Ops Roundtable Virtual Events. We have a segment called Women in Retail Automotive during these events, which is very popular. During the last event, the panelists spoke about the lack of women in leadership positions in automotive dealerships.

On the first day of training at Saturn Corporation, we got to know each other very creatively through an activity called Three Facts and a Fib. The trainer's name was Carolyn Warren. Carolyn was an experienced trainer, and she was passionate about the Saturn brand and life.

Saturn led the way years ago by including women in leadership at every level of their operation. Jill Lajdziak was the general manager for Saturn Corporation in 2004. She was one of if not the first woman to be put in charge of an automotive company. Aside from being named one of the 100 Leading Women in the North American Auto Industry in 2005, she didn't get much recognition for it like women do today.

Having women in charge was unique to the world, and uncommon in the car business. My dealership had women in sales, sales management, finance management, and service management roles. Saturn has always been ahead of its time in automotive.

MILE MARKER

Ensure your work environment is fun, engaging, and offers a diverse work experience that promotes personal growth and understanding for every team member. When you do training, use a variety of methods because different people learn different ways.

SEVENTEEN

MILE SEVENTEEN – SHARE YOUR GOALS AND IGNORE THE SCOFFERS

UPON RETURNING TO THE DEALERSHIP, everyone wanted to hear my Saturn stories. But the story they weren't excited to hear was the one about my goal of becoming a Saturn trainer. It wasn't as if anyone worried about me leaving the company; they just wondered how my ego could be so large as to have the audacity to think I could join such an elite team of trainers. It's as if an enlisted guy had said, "I'm going to be a Navy SEAL!"

The Timothy figure from the Bible represented more of my work personality type to this point in my life. He is known for being a timid leader. My new behavior was like James and John, who were called "the sons of thunder" in scripture. They got the other disciples upset when they asked Jesus to promote them after they all got to heaven. Some gall! As it turned out, almost everyone on our team wanted to work for Saturn Corporation. Several sales consultants and managers dreamed about becoming trainers for Saturn, so my attitude came off as somewhat arrogant. It's interesting to note that Jesus told James and John the positions had already been filled. But he didn't disparage them for asking the question or dreaming the dream.

As you might expect, others immediately told me why someone like me could never make it as a Saturn trainer. Not enough experience in sales. No automotive management experience, and no advanced degree. None of that stopped me from pursuing the dream. When you have a vision, or a goal, find out what it takes to achieve it. Unless it's unattainable, go for it. It felt like the spirit was upon me, and I was acting like a son of thunder! I picked up the phone and called Saturn.

Fortunately, one of Saturn's lead trainers, Joe Jordan, took my call. Of all the people you could ever meet professionally, Joe is one of the most encouraging and supportive. He treats everyone the same way. Joe was the first person I'd met who called both men and women, "Buddy." It was his way of showing respect and an attitude of equality.

Joe explained to me more experience in sales and sales management would be necessary. He said finance management would be helpful. So, we agreed to stay in touch, and I would let him know how things were going. It would likely be a few years before Saturn would consider me, provided a position opened up. Joe would continue to play a significant role in my journey, and we are still friends today. Thanks, Joe, for being my "wingman!"

MILE MARKER

Have clear goals. Share them with others and make a plan to accomplish them. Know and write down the obstacles you need to overcome and list the people you need to connect with to help you along the way. Set a deadline and list the benefits you will receive once you arrive at your destination.

EIGHTEEN

MILE EIGHTEEN – ALWAYS BE READY TO ACT

MY CONVICTION WAS DEFINITE. Becoming a Saturn trainer was simply a matter of time. Don't ask me how, but my mind was sure one day this previously shy little boy would become a member of the Saturn Retail Training Team.

A few months after my return from Spring Hill, General Motors became the first manufacturer in the US to sell electric vehicles to consumers on a mass scale. They chose Saturn as the dealership group to market and sell the EV1. The EV1 project created a variety of positions both inside and outside the retail facilities. As the lead sales consultant in the store, and as one who had a technical background, the role of EV specialist was offered to me. A few months later, I joined several other EV specialists in Pomona, California, to receive training on the GM EV1 electric vehicle.

The EV1 was a very cool car. It accelerated more smoothly and more quickly than any car I'd ever driven. Some of the things we learned (and eventually taught others) would help me decades later during the development and delivery of training for Mitsubishi Outlander's PHEV, the first plug-in hybrid electric SUV in the world.

The Saturn facilitator for the training was Chris Saraceno. Unlike the first Saturn trainer I'd seen, Chris, like Carolyn, set the bar extremely high. These trainers were terrific, and my skills were nowhere near where they needed to be by comparison. But nothing would stop me from working the plan. At the first break of the morning, I approached Chris and told him about my goal of becoming a Saturn trainer. Only Chris knows what he was thinking at the time, but as trainers, we were regularly approached by salespeople asking us how they can do what we do. In this case, "how" wasn't a question; I just wanted someone else to know.

Maybe it was my approach, or perhaps it was just a feeling he had. Or maybe Chris was just calling my bluff. Then again, the scripture says, "A man makes his plans, but the Lord straightens the path." If you commit your plans to the Lord, and He blesses those plans, they will come to pass. Some people say you reap what you sow, and others will tell you it's the law of attraction. Whatever you believe, Chris may not have had a choice (wink, wink).

Rather than blow me off, Chris offered me the opportunity to take the next step in my goal. He gave me his leader guide and told me to read up on the first section of the afternoon training. "After lunch," Chris said, "you'll do the first section...If you want to?"

I guess some people would have freaked out, had stage fright, or just plain got sick to their stomach. Not me. I was brought up in the home of an entertainer. Being on stage or around a camera most of my life has made public speaking somewhat easy for me compared to most, and it appears to be how God works. He puts you in situations and prepares you for what He's called you to do.

When lunchtime came, I grabbed a sandwich, sat down, and dug into the material. One of the other sales consultants asked me what was up. He thought it was crazy. But thirty minutes later, I was standing in front of my peers, explaining the features and benefits of an electric car I'd only learned a few minutes earlier. What a gas!

In fairness, learning stuff fast wasn't new to me—one time when I was teaching junior high school, the Spanish teacher got sick at lunch and the only teacher available to substitute was yours truly. There was only an hour to learn how to tell the time in Spanish and determine the pronunciation. But it all worked out. The students had no idea what I knew or didn't know, and it was a lot of fun teaching the class. The same was true in my first-day training Saturn sales consultants, even though the Saturn facilitator title was a few years away.

Chris was either impressed or shocked at my willingness to do it at all. He called Saturn corporate and spoke to Joe Jordan about what happened. There was still a lot to accomplish, but the EV1 opportunity turned into gold for me and my future with Saturn. Chris and I are connected to this day on LinkedIn. He's a fantastic person, incredible car guy, family man, VP and partner at Kelly Automotive, and author of a book I highly recommend called *The Theory of 5*. Thanks, Chris, for what you did for me, and who you are today!

MILE MARKER

Be prepared to answer the call when opportunity knocks. Be willing to take personal risks to achieve your goals.

NINETEEN

MILE NINETEEN – WORK THE PLAN

TWO YEARS after my automotive sales career began, an offer to become finance manager came, and there was no hesitation to accept. This offer was both a natural next step toward my goal and one which made sense to the dealership. My per-unit average for finance and total gross profit was typically the highest among the top three of the four stores in the group every month. It also gave me the added benefit of being home every other weekend.

One of many things I learned in finance was that lenders make stupid rules sometimes. In most cases, they set things up to mitigate risks to the detriment of doing any business. In other cases, they created rules to "simplify" the process for dealers and customers, only to shoot themselves in the foot. The most famous instance of all time (in my opinion) was the 0-0-0 financing offered by Mitsubishi Motor Credit in the early 2000s. It ended up costing them $672 million in losses, from which they have yet to recover.

In another situation, Chase Auto Finance offered a simple one-page checklist that allowed a finance manager to confirm all the stipulations were met, pack up the contract with the list, and send it in. One Monday morning, I came into my office after a weekend off and I noticed a declined deal from Chase. My partner had run only the husband's credit because the wife worked part-time, making less per month than the car payment. The loan was declined because the debt-to-income ratio was slightly out of whack, but the applicant had never been late on anything, and he was a skilled welder with a stable work history.

Knowing how things worked, I ran the credit on the wife and found she met all the requirements of the Chase approval form WITHOUT using the husband. There was no income requirement!! I removed the husband from the contract. I called the customer and had the wife sign the new documents. Then I sent it to Chase. Boy, was the buyer from Chase unhappy with me. They wanted to send it back, but I followed their rules, so they were stuck with it. These are the types of experiences I needed to later engage with finance managers, and it was all part of the plan.

When you have a plan and work it, you're better able to take alternate or new routes that appear before you because you're actually on the road toward your destination. If you only have a vision, but you don't have the journey mapped out, you're less likely to get started, and you're not expected to arrive at the destination you're dreaming of visiting.

Then another opportunity opened up to me, which, frankly, wasn't expected. The dealership offered me a job as a part-time corporate trainer.

MILE MARKER
Work each step of the plan as you have laid it out. Set a

goal but focus on the process. The journey is where the magic happens.

TWENTY

MILE TWENTY – PAY IT-FORWARD

BESIDES THE FACT that everyone knew my goal, my philosophy was different from that of most top performers in sales. Other "superstars" at dealerships hid their sales secrets from other salespeople. They felt threatened and thought if they shared too much, they might get knocked off their perch. That philosophy never made sense to me, and my two fantastic managers knew how things worked.

Dennis and Becky were both supportive and wise leaders. They explained to me the energy in the entire store picks up, and everyone does better as more cars are sold. It made sense to me. When an idea worked, my default action was to share it with the team. Dennis asked me to sit down with others on occasion and coach them, especially when it came to the interview. Because of my willingness to share, and when others improved, it made sense for management to offer me the trainer's job.

I was particularly adept at two of the seven sales process

steps: the facility tour (part of the welcome) and the interview. I learned how to perform a facility tour from my pastor years ago. He told the story of his best friend who sold cars. Immediately after greeting a customer on the lot, he would say, "Come with me!" He would then show them around by letting them know the buying process was short compared to the owning experience. Who took care of them after the sale was more important, wouldn't you agree? All my customers did!

Most salespeople followed a fact-finding process that was more of an interrogation than a discussion. It was a series of quick, closed-ended questions that targeted a specific model and trim, but not how a customer experienced using their car. In one particular situation, I asked a customer, "What is most important in your next car?" To which the customer replied, "Comfort!" Most salespeople would not follow that up with, "What does comfort mean to you?" but I did, to which he described how the ergonomics of the vehicle were significant during his long trips. It made all the difference in how I sold cars.

As a result, I coached most existing salespeople on the tour and interview steps, while also taking all new salespeople through every step of orientation and the sales process. On my days off, the store would pay me a hundred and fifty dollars to train new hires in Saturn culture, and the consultative sales process. It helped me gain experience as a trainer, but it also helped me refine my selling skills and improve my finance performance. There's an old saying, "If you want to learn something, teach it."

There's a scripture that helped me during this time of success. It says, "Humble yourself before the Lord, and He will exalt you." My progress wasn't the result of my efforts alone, or my own decisions impacting my future. Others around me had a vital role to play. Accountability and continuous improvement were essential to my success, and my team leaders helped me a lot with those areas of my life. There were several times my zealousness and drive caused me to lose sight of others around me. Coaching was needed, and, frankly, it still can be an issue. The only solution is humility. Listening to others' concerns and accepting that my actions aren't always the best for everyone around me has been an important lesson to learn.

MILE MARKER

Be willing to help others succeed without any expectation of getting something back. Give yourself to others in need. Approach each day with humility and an understanding that the way you approach success may not benefit everyone.

TWENTY-ONE

MILE TWENTY-ONE – GAIN NEW SKILLS WHILE WAITING FOR THE CALL

THE FINANCE DEPARTMENT WAS FUN. There were more people more often, and it required some skills yet developed. There were days when we would sell a car at midnight, and I wouldn't get home until 3 a.m. We were required to balance the doc sheet before leaving the store, so if it wasn't accurate, we stayed until it was right. It all worked out, though, because they gave me my own set of keys to the store.

My role in the position of finance manager lasted about six months. Then one day, the phone rang. It was Joe Jordan from Saturn. We had kept in touch, but this call was different. It wasn't a job offer, but it was an opportunity that opened several doors for me. You see, Joe had recommended me to a magazine called *Sales and Marketing Management*. In the October 1998 issue, Sarah Lorge wrote an article about me called, "Highway to Heaven."

This magazine was no "one-off" issue: Michael Dell graced the cover, and the issue was titled "Top 25 Sales Forces in America" and Saturn just happened to come in at number 13. When Joe told me he'd given my name to Sarah, I was both dumbfounded and highly honored. The article began, "With nothing more than his faith in the Saturn Sales Process..." and went on to tell the story of how a former minister sold a lot of cars honestly and ethically.

While the article alone didn't propel me into the automotive stratosphere, it did bring me a level of credibility not as yet achieved. My confidence and degree of certainty of being on track to reach my goal went into orbit. I'm not sure if it helped me land a position on Saturn's retail training team; only Joe and the others who made the decision know for sure. One thing is certain: It didn't hurt.

MILE MARKER

Always improve your skills, and you'll be recognized because of it. Focus on the details to become the best you can be, then you'll be ready for whatever comes your way.

TWENTY-TWO

MILE TWENTY-TWO – GOALS CAN BE ACHIEVED

NOT LONG AFTER the article hit the newsstand (yes, they still had those back then), there was another call from Joe. This time it was THE call. From the first visit to Springhill, and my first experience with Saturn culture, I was hooked. If my calling wasn't a full-time evangelist for God, my second choice was to be part of a company with a vision to treat people with honesty, integrity, and respect. I could be who I wanted to be and help others be successful too.

An interview was set, and a trip was needed to fly to Nashville. Saturn paid for the trip, which was five hours there, an hour and a half with the interview team at the Nashville International Airport in a meeting room within the terminal, and five hours back. I prepared a presentation as requested, and my speaking, training, and coaching experience paid off. I did okay.

It felt like a month before the call came from Saturn, but it was only a week. Memory fails me now as to whether it was Joe who called, but I practically peed myself. I was sitting in the finance office at the time, and my reaction was to hang up the phone and let out a quiet but audible yelp.

The walk to Dennis' office was brisk. Were my feet actually on the ground? He looked at me like a proud father who was about to lose his son to college. But it was bittersweet. We'd had some fantastic times together, and they were going to be missed. One crucial thing remained.

It was the policy at Saturn not to hire anyone from a retail partner without a signed agreement in the form of an official letter from the dealer. I wasn't worried, but I had to rely on my general manager's willingness to lose a top performer to allow me to live my dream. It couldn't have gone any better. Steve (my GM) was so excited for me and even said by helping the company as a whole, it would be assisting the dealership. No wonder this organization was, and always will be, an example of great leadership.

I had been on quite a journey. I had hoped that things would happen more rapidly, but everything fell into place exactly as it should. Remember, diamonds require a lot of time and a great deal of pressure to convert them from a lump of coal to a beautiful gem. One Psalm says, "Wait for the Lord; be strong, and let your heart take courage; wait for the Lord."

THE TRIP DOWN SATURN WAY

I had the opportunity to work with Saturn directly as a trainer for a combined four years. It's sad when I bring Saturn up, tell stories of things I'm proud of, and all Saturn accomplished, and I hear someone say, "Well, Saturn's out of business!" Typically, that comment comes from someone at a

GM dealership or the UAW who facilitated Saturn's demise and continues to speak negatively about the Saturn brand.

Automotive writers thoroughly documented the reasons Saturn is out of business. The articles are easy to find. I had close connections inside Saturn and GM at the time, so I know what happened. The Different Kind of Company isn't gone because of its strategy, vision, or original leadership. It wasn't due to a lack of sales. It had to do with an attitude of jealousy among other General Motors brands and union leadership. Saturn was a threat, pure and simple.

What's interesting to me, especially in the world of automotive, is today, more and more companies are implementing strategies that were standard, everyday stuff at Saturn. The Saturn values have been rewritten and repurposed to provide exceptional customer experiences in more ways, and with more companies, than any other sales process with which I'm familiar. How many other automotive companies have had college courses written about their business model and customer strategy?

I will continue to defend Saturn's reputation and the things Saturn stood for to their employees and their customers. I repurposed their materials for other manufacturers and helped turn their SSI (sales) and CSI (Customer Satisfaction Index) around significantly due to Saturn's strategies. Sadly, they weren't able to sustain those ideas because you have to get buy-in throughout an organization to maintain success.

The Saturn values included:

- Commitment to Customer Enthusiasm
- Commitment to Excel
- Trust and Respect for the Individual
- Teamwork

THE MILES AND THE MARKERS 63

- *Commitment to Continuous Improvement*

Strategies like no hassle - no haggle, cash values for trade-ins, and 30-day money back guarantee were put in place to create a level of enthusiasm unequaled even by luxury brands. These values are similar to the principles I train with the FISH! Philosophy®.

People forget how Saturn came to be. They don't remember the story about "The Group of 99" and all their research. The two-million hours invested with customers and dealers made Saturn unique.

I have never heard of a manufacturer that consistently topped the JD power SSI index and the CSI index for five consecutive years except for Saturn. But when GM tried to convert Saturn back to the traditional model, Skip Lefauve (Saturn's then-president) responded with something like, "Everyone else should adapt to the way we do business rather than us adapting to the way they do business." And he was right.

Since the early days of Saturn, other luxury brands like Lexus have adopted elements of Saturn's Consultative Sales Process. Once they did, they returned (as any expensive product should) to the top of the SSI and CSI list. But instead of listening to Skip, GM promoted him right out of Saturn and sent him to Europe where he couldn't cause trouble.

It's sad how petty jealousy and attitudes of superiority led to the demise of a brand millions of people embraced. Here's the real tragedy: Not much has changed in the automotive industry since then. Oh, there have been a few "attempts." But you can't take a jackrabbit and ask it to act like an eagle. The automotive industry is more of a caterpillar needing to become a butterfly, but it refuses to climb the tree to make the cocoon. There has to be a metamorphosis for change to occur. Every aspect of leadership and processes needs to change at the cellular level. Covid-19 may sadly be the catalyst that forces the industry to behave the way customers want them to act. I'm still not convinced the auto industry will change.

Major manufacturers still play by the same rule book they've played under for decades. While small businesses have to operate by different rules, major automotive manufacturers get special privileges from governments, and they continue to act as if the consumer owes them something. This type of attitude filters down to dealerships and causes them to play by unethical, unfair, and sometimes illegal rules. Union bosses still manipulate both manufactures and their members to stay in power.

Today's consumers are tired of the nonsense. Of course, as I write this, we're battling a national shutdown due to Covid-19. And because automotive manufacturers are uniquely tooled and able to provide things like ventilators and masks to the federal government, they're all praised as heroic. They are not heroes. If they had any choice in the matter, most automotive companies wouldn't do it. The work many are doing on behalf of the pandemic is a political move and nothing more.

In 2008, an opportunity to diversify my client portfolio came up. But the training partner I worked for under contract with General Motors complained how badly they needed me to continue working for GM alone. As a result, I made the mistake of agreeing to provide 100% of my work to General Motors.

Four months later, and the day before General Motors received $17 billion from the federal government, I received a call canceling all of my contracts. There was no recourse to *receive any money (due to me under the cancellation agreement) because General Motors filed for bankruptcy. Others suffered too. Yet, as a Christian, we're about love, acceptance, and forgiveness. It's important to consider what we do with others' pain, whether an individual or a company.*

It may seem like I'm bitter toward General Motors, and I suppose if one could be angry, I would certainly have the right to be. I'm not. It was Roger Smith and General Motors, who created Saturn and, indirectly, my career. For that, I'm grateful. On the other hand, books like J. Patrick Wright's "On a Clear Day You Can See General Motors" blew the lid off the automotive giant's inner workings back in the late 1970s, and it appears those attitudes have never entirely left the culture.

I hope this part of the story will encourage consumers to rise and demand experiences based on their wants and needs rather than the needs of board members, governments, union leaders, and a few unethical dealerships. Customers have the power of the purse. They don't have to buy products from companies continuing to leverage them through manipulation and gamesmanship. Find a company and a dealership who treats you with integrity, honesty, transparency, and respect. Do business with them and leave the rest behind. That is the only way to change the industry. It's up to the consumer to demand it and force its stock value to plummet. If you continue to be willing to do business the way of the horse trader and the caveman, don't expect car companies or dealers to change.

MILE MARKER

Understand what motivates you and why you do what you do. Leverage this to ensure you're on the right path toward achieving your goals. If you believe it, you will act upon it.

TWENTY-THREE

MILE TWENTY-THREE – EXPECT AND BE READY FOR CHANGE

WHEN YOU SET a goal and work the plan, it can become a reality. The first flight to Nashville was on a Sunday afternoon. Traveling for work is not the adventure most people think it is. Single folks make it into a mini-vacation or an opportunity to explore. Some married trainers do too. The work can be rewarding, but don't take the impact travel can have on you and your family lightly.

There have been the same day flights to cities within my state and the big trips to places like Japan for Mazda's development work. There are good flights and bad ones—great rental cars and clunkers. There are five-star hotels and ones with bed bugs. My luggage made it most of the time, and only once did I lose a piece of expensive equipment I needed for training. Travel has been mainly part of the job for me, and rarely an adventure. It has been a necessary part of the work I do. Now that I've been home for most of the last year, I don't miss it one bit.

Given what's happening in the world today, most of us will need to figure out how to do our jobs remotely or figure out a new career—maybe writing a book? Perhaps two or more books. In any case, my entire adult life has been coaching, facilitating, or educating young people, customers, and adults on how to improve their lives and make a better living. Nothing brings greater joy in life than helping others learn and become better human beings.

That said, life is always changing. We don't like it, and we typically avoid it. We want consistency, even if it means things aren't good for us. We're more afraid of change than we are a life of discomfort or even fear as long as we know what to expect every day. The unknown stops many people from taking a risk that could prove to be the best thing.

MILE MARKER

Be prepared for change. Count the cost. Know it won't be easy, but understand it will come, and be ready when it happens. Since change is inevitable, you can try to run from it, or get excited about what the future holds.

TWENTY-FOUR

A SIDE STREET CALLED INTRINSIC MOTIVATION

SOMETHING MUST BE SAID about a challenge that came from my recent LinkedIn post called, "I'm a Car Guy." One of the people who responded to the post asked, "If the job paid eight bucks an hour, would you do it?" In all honesty, no. But there is more to why most of us do what we do than money. Maybe it's a passion for helping others learn. Perhaps you want success to have more free time. Whatever your motivation, people need to understand it. Employers need to reward it rather than just throw money at good people.

The skills and experience required to be considered credible as a trainer or business consultant are significant. Walk into a dealership when you've never sold or serviced cars, and they will sniff you out, eat you up, and spit you onto the sidewalk. Try teaching managers how to manage if you've never walked in their shoes, and things get ugly fast. You may be able to fake it in the short term, but your reputation will precede you. The job pays a lot because it deserves to be paid a lot.

TWENTY-FIVE

MILE TWENTY-FOUR – LEARNING REQUIRES INVOLVEMENT AND COACHING

THE FIRST DAY as a Saturn facilitator included me observing a master trainer named Charlie Brown! No kidding! Charlie was anything but a guy with low self-esteem who paid a nickel for psychological counseling from Lucy. He was an experienced automotive professional who understood team building, customer experiences, and "The Saturn Way." Charlie came from the old-school of automotive. He knew what a difference training could make on the lives of those in the room.

Charlie showed me what it was like to command a room while facilitating learning. Yes, he was a trainer. But he demonstrated how to help others discover the teaching. Charlie was the first person to teach me the concept made famous by Ben Franklin: "Tell me, and I'll forget, show me, and I'll learn, involve me, and I'll understand."

It reminded me of another concept taught to me by

author Jim Burns. It was a different concept about discipleship, but somewhat similar. "I'll do it, and you watch, you do it, and I'll watch, you do it, and I'll go do something else." The bottom line is people don't learn by just hearing us talk. Why do so many sales meetings, lessons, and webinars not engage with the learner? Adult learning theory has been around for decades, yet instructors' default to what's easy for them, rather than what is best for the student.

The next day it was my turn. My facilitation began in the afternoon session with both Charlie and Joe Jordan looking on. They let me plow through the material without interruption, allowing me to struggle but still get through the content. Had I messed up, they would have been able to jump in and save the day for the participants, but things went well enough, and it wasn't necessary.

When the day ended, Joe and Charlie walked through a review process I still use today. It's called "Plus, Minus, and Interesting." Plus uses the (+) symbol and identifies commendable things. It was a pleasant surprise to see most of the comments fell into this category. It was a strategic and essential lesson to learn when evaluating talent. Focusing on the positives is vital to encouraging personal growth in others. The latest studies involving learning suggest learning that is skewed slightly to the positive is retained far better than neutral or negative reinforcement.

Next came the minus (-) section. Listed here were opportunities to improve. One of the big ones was my use of the word "um." I used "um" as a filler any time I didn't know what to say or felt nervous. Rather than simply pause, "um" came out of my mouth. They counted 65 times in four hours that I said the word, "um."

The beautiful thing about having coaches to help identify opportunities like this is the next time you make a mistake, it's as if a loudspeaker goes off in your head, reminding you, "You did it again!" If memory serves me well, the word "um" came out a few times the next morning, but by the afternoon, the term "um," rang in my head long before it came out of my mouth. I stopped saying it. Now you see the value of feedback! Feedback is nothing to fear. Instead, it is something we should all cherish.

Jesus' disciples followed Him for three years. Learning and understanding require a commitment and dedication to following philosophies and teachings proven over time. It isn't just about the teacher. Jonathan Gobel, CEO of Charthouse Learning, has led change at several large and smaller hospitals. He says real change takes a CEO five years to make it stick. That may seem like a long time, but what is your purpose?

There's a famous saying: "When the student is ready, the teacher will appear." There are plenty of mentors, teachers, and coaches ready and willing to help and support. The first step is to have a willing attitude and a mind hungry to learn and accept coaching.

CORPORATE TRAINING BOULEVARD

Hardly anyone invests fully in training today. Budgets have been slashed, staff sizes trimmed, and strategic processes have been all but eliminated in favor of technology, marketing gimmicks, and quick fixes. Training departments are more about firefighting than fire prevention. Imagine if the fire department never inspected equipment or trained their team on how to put out a fire. Now imagine if the fire chief began lighting the flames and the firefighters had to extinguish them. You get the idea of what much of the corporate world is like, especially in automotive.

Our training team (and others) used to follow a strict process of development, including a project manager, a writer, a subject matter expert, and a lead trainer. The lead trainer would pilot the project with real participants, gain feedback, and make corrections. The pilot was followed by a T-3 (Train-The-Trainer) for those delivering the materials, who would observe the complete training in real-time. Next were teach-back sessions, and then a team teach with either the project manager, the lead trainer, or the lead writer in attendance. The entire process to be certified to teach a new class took a minimum of three weeks. Today it's not uncommon to receive a leader guide via FedEx and be expected to deliver training the following week, with no coaching and nobody modeling the expectation. Current training processes are absurd, and the corporate world should be ashamed for slashing their training budgets. There is a proverb that says, "you reap what you sow:" This will eventually come back to haunt corporations that do not adequately train their people.

Over the week, Charlie and I "team-taught" the class. It was awesome. There was so much to learn, and one can never replace the value of the learning and coaching received throughout the years from trainers and mentors like Charlie and Joe. Twenty-plus years later, they are still in my life, offering feedback and advice. I love all my Saturn Team!

MILE MARKER

Get a coach. Find someone to help identify your opportunities to improve, and to help you process your decisions. Also, mentor others who need your experience and insight.

TWENTY-SIX

MILE TWENTY-FIVE – FAITH AND BUSINESS CAN ALIGN

LANDING MY "DREAM" job didn't mean my life became more comfortable. My life wasn't instantly better, and I wasn't automatically a happier person because of a dream fulfilled. Life is complex. Family relationships, responsibilities, and living a life of faith are all challenged daily. The difficulty we all face is how to make a difference in the world. As a Christian, I still wondered how to make a difference for the Kingdom of God. How could I do this while respecting my role as a servant to others who may not believe?

In the business world and social settings apart from the church, you're expected to avoid topics such as politics, religion, sex, race, or any other issue which could generate an argument or push back. It is interesting Christianity is considered taboo in certain circles, while other religions are acceptable and even favored topics of discussion in America. We believers in Christ don't have a particular dress or hairstyle differentiating us like some religions, at least not in the west. In a way, others can share their faith by how they dress, cover their heads, or wear their hair or beard.

On the other hand, Christians can't openly express their faith because it is somehow deemed offensive. Since when did grace, mercy, hope, charity, love, acceptance, and forgiveness become problematic? Maybe it's similar to the way car dealers have a reputation for dishonesty. They created shady lease deals and underhanded finance practices in the 60s and 70s. Similarly, Christianity carries baggage from hellfire and brimstone preachers. Their message at the well-documented revival tent meetings was fear and wrath from above. When you add to it the changes in society related to sexuality, the right to choose, and other government involvement in our lives, it seems Christians need to walk a fine line. For me, working at Saturn made this simple.

Each of the Saturn values can be associated with a verse or behavior promoted by Christ and his disciples. In a letter written to the Philippian Church, for example, Paul writes, "Finally, brothers and sisters, whatever is true, whatever is noble, whatever is right, whatever is pure, whatever is lovely, whatever is admirable–if anything is excellent or praiseworthy–think about such things." At Saturn, we changed the language of the car business. "Deal" became "agreement," "customer" became "guest," and so on.

But the car business, in general, is still made up of mostly men. Men are attracted to the industry because they can make money quickly with little or no formal education. I'm not knocking anyone's intelligence mind you; on the contrary, those who navigate their way into sales management are required to learn skills equivalent to what most learn in a typical MBA program. But the mindset of at least half of them is more like what you'd find in a men's locker room than in church.

There are crass jokes, foul language, and celebrations whenever they successfully maximized their gross profits, regardless of the benefit to the customer. It still surprises me how many men in our industry use the "F" word and other curse words as if it's somehow an expected norm to show others you are a man. Frankly, I don't get it. The vulgarity of any kind is entirely unnecessary. If my efforts in the car business accomplish nothing more than changing the majority of men's language, then it will have been worth it. If this book results in the elimination of the "F" bomb or the "S" word from the ordinary discourse of terms being used by car guys (and a few gals), then my mission will have been a success!

You need to know that I'm in favor of profitability and making money. Christianity supports being a wise and good steward of money. But taking advantage of people for no other reason than to line our pocketbooks isn't something to be celebrated. It isn't considered to be ethical, and it's frowned upon in scripture too. Nevertheless, these are the things we have to contend with as both automotive professionals and as Christians.

MILE MARKER

Whether you believe in a personal God or not, you know there is something outside yourself and beyond your control. Seek to understand the unseen things in life to learn and grow beyond your five senses. You will become a better person for yourself and others.

TWENTY-SEVEN

MILE TWENTY-SIX – REPRESENT WHEREVER YOU ARE

ARE you the same person at home, on the road, in an office, at the gym, or when you're communicating on social media? Do your travel plans include changing who you are once you leave town? There have been lots of acquaintances who behaved one way at home or in the office, but another way entirely once they hit the road. Acting like a different person when you are away from the office or home can be detrimental to you personally and professionally.

Here's something to consider: When you act differently on the road than when you are at home, you put others around you in a compromising position. The corporate world is a small one. Most people at work interact with family members at some point in your career. Is it worth the negative outcome to be one person on the road and someone else at home or the office?

Nobody is perfect. It's crucial, then, that you define

your values and your standards for life and business before you crawl out of bed every morning. Having an accountability partner could be helpful to you if you travel for work. It's great if it can be your spouse or significant other, but that doesn't always work.

There's nothing worse in my mind than having people tell stories about your adventures behind your back because of moral failures. Far too many marriages, families, businesses, and careers have crumbled due to poor judgment and a lack of being honest with yourself and others. Take up the challenge to represent ethical values and moral integrity wherever you are.

MILE MARKER

Be the same person at home, at work, at church, or when you're playing on the golf course. Always represent a person of strength, courage, and good character. Your character is a choice you make. You don't have to be religious to be a good human being. But you do have to represent well wherever you are to finish well.

TWENTY-EIGHT

MILE TWENTY-SEVEN – RETURN TO FACE NEW CHALLENGES

JUST UNDER TWO years after traveling almost weekly, a call came from my former dealer asking me to consider taking the position of service manager for their new Saab franchise. They had been through three service managers in the first nine months, and they were building a new store. "These guys understand everything about the Saab product, but they have no idea how to treat customers," was the message from Dennis.

Additionally, 90-day warranty claims weren't correctly filed, and all the work was being done out of a Saturn facility 15 miles away from the Saab dealership. Customers were dropping their cars off at both locations, but all were being serviced or repaired at Saturn of Huntington Beach. Being on the road took a toll on the family, so I agreed to take the job.

What followed was a year of adventure, which taught

me many lessons about technology, team leadership, service management, and customer experience. This year was one of the more significant times of personal growth in my life. I was thrown into the fire and expected to turn around a department last in the district in CSI while maintaining profitability.

One big challenge was we were piloting a new Windows-based software system, and the T1 lines connecting the two stores was smack in the middle of two different phone system providers. When the hub went down, we lost connection between the two stores, causing us to handwrite all the repair orders. The lines went down at least once a month. When they did, I was required to drive to the Saab dealership after hours and input all the repair orders into the system. Sometimes my head hit the pillow well after midnight.

Another experience included a time when we had to fire a customer. You read it right! We had a customer who was so ill-tempered and treated my staff with such disrespect, the general manager and I worked out a deal to buy her out of her car. We paid full retail for it, but trust me, and it was worth it. Never in my management career has more praise been heaped upon me from a group I managed than the day I freed them from the abuse they'd experienced for nearly six months.

A few months after the store was completed, my dealer asked me to move into sales management, but my response was less than favorable. Their reasoning was sound. They needed a sales manager, but there was also a candidate for service manager who was better qualified than I was. Still, it felt as if there was no choice, and I set a meeting with the dealer principal to discuss it.

If there was ever a time when my trust in God didn't

show up, it was now. I lashed out at someone I highly respected and suggested he'd taken advantage of me. I'd given up a highly sought-after position with Saturn to come and bail him out of a tough situation. Now he was asking me to give up something I'd built. I even went so far as to swear at him. And though it wasn't directed at him, it was one of the few times I completely lost my cool. In retrospect, I'm fortunate he still wanted me to stay with the company. But he did. And some fantastic opportunities came as a result of the move.

Job moves and changes can be difficult. Christians are taught that "God causes all things to work for good for those who love Him and are called to according to His purpose." This idea is in stark contrast to the non-biblical phrase, "God helps those who help themselves." That is not in the Bible. But if it means God has made soil for seed, and if you don't plant, you won't reap, then I agree with that in principle. But most use it as a boast to suggest they've done the work that you haven't, so God blessed them for it. If we trust God, we should know He always has our best interest in mind, and something good will come from anything we face in life. Having this mindset is what makes walking with Jesus unique. In every experience in my life, God has always opened doors of opportunity and personal growth for me.

MILE MARKER

Be fearless, but not vindictive. Look at the next challenge as an opportunity to grow and become better than you are today.

TWENTY-NINE

MILE TWENTY-EIGHT - FIND YOUR PURPOSE

BY NOW, it may be apparent to you my calling has been to start new things. My wife and I have launched several ministries for churches, started several companies, and my personal experience has led to me helping departments transition, or begin new strategies within an organization. The exciting thing is, at 62 years old, I didn't understand this about myself until I started writing this book and reflecting on where life has taken me. Had I known who I was and my strengths and gifts, I wouldn't have put up such a fuss when I was asked to give up the job as service manager. Another new opportunity was just around the corner.

Before we move on to the next step in my journey, it's important to remember that employees and clients are people first and foremost. Shortly after taking the sales manager position at Saab, a man came in and parked his six-month-old Silver 9-3 Saab Sedan, exited quickly, then turned toward our showroom with a look of sadness on his face. For the sake of this story, I'll call him Jim.

After I greeted Jim, he extended his arm with two sets of key fobs in his hand and said, "I need you to take these. I need you to take my car." As I listened, Jim explained that he had come at once from the body shop after they'd completed the repairs to the front end and windshield of his car just hours ago. "Two weeks ago," he said, "I was driving along the coast in the morning. It was foggy that day, and a twelve-year-old boy with a surfboard strapped to his bike came flying down the hill in front of me. Whether he lost control or just didn't see me, I don't know."

At this point, Jim began to sob openly. "I killed him. I hit him with my car, and I killed him. I need you to take this car. Please just take it."

This story is an example of the real people we work with daily. American author Brad Metzler has been attributed with the quote, "Everyone is fighting a battle you know nothing about. Be kind, always." We must remember this as we encounter our clients and work with our team members. There is always a back story that could help us explain them a little better. We need to be understanding, patient, and good listeners. We never know who we might be able to help.

I helped Jim get a new car that day. He was grateful for how our team supported him, and we all saw how relieved he was as he drove away. We spoke a several times over the next few years and he sounded like he'd worked through much of pain. I consider it an honor to have been there to help him in his time of despair.

After six months of successful sales management at Saab (which included the development of brand-new finance and after sales program), the call came to return to Saturn to help manage the sales team and oversee onboarding new hires. It was at this time I was reintroduced to the FISH! Philosophy®. Three months afterward, my job was overseeing a brand-new Business Development Center (BDC) for all the Saturn of Orange County locations, including managing a staff taking all inbound calls for sales and service. We made all outbound sales and service calls for campaigns, recalls, and appointment confirmations.

When the BDC first launched, we worked with a software company to develop a customized program specifically for our company. During this time, several amazing people would come to the dealership to see what was going on with our BDC, including folks like Les Silver who, along with my good friend John Traver, is known in automotive circles as a pioneer in BDC and CRM solutions, and indeed they are.

MILE MARKER

Know your "why" so well that when detours or obstacles appear, you are not discouraged. You make the needed adjustments and continue toward your destination. You also treat everyone with respect, as they may be hiding a secret pain.

THIRTY

MILE TWENTY-NINE – WORDS ARE POWERFUL TOOLS

ONE OF THE essential things developed during this adventure was the proper training and the power of scripts. At Traver Connect call center they're known as call guides. When utilized correctly, scripts (or word-tracks) can make a massive difference in your team's success or failure. The challenge comes when team members aren't managed successfully, or when leadership doesn't know how to train team members how to use scripts effectively. The outsourcing of customer service has been detrimental to the use and acceptance of scripts in the automotive world. It's rare to find someone in another country capable of having a conversation in English apart from using a script. They tend to default to reading words on their screen, and their delivery sounds canned.

When training on scripts, my approach is to ask participants who their favorite actor or actress is. Then we discuss what character played by the actor was their favorite one. You can see where this is going: "One of my favorite actors is Tom Hanks. Tom Hanks is not Forrest Gump! But he won an Oscar because he made all of us believe he was Forrest Gump!" Afterward, we discuss the process the cast goes through to prepare for their role. Trust me; it's a lot of work. It begins just reading the script sitting around a table. Then they memorize the story and start practicing the delivery. Long after comes the blocking or moving around in character along with saying the lines. It's a process.

Sadly, too many new sales folks read a script and say, "That's just not me!" My response is, who are you? Were you born talking? Are the words you say words you invented? Were you the originator of all the phrases you use today, or did you copy someone else? The way you talk, and most of the words you use resulted from things programmed into your brain subconsciously by listening to your parents or your friends talk. Your words are learned, and you can learn how to make scripts become you.

The Bible insists Christians should "study to show yourself approved," and "be transformed by the renewing of your mind." This means believers in Jesus should read and align with **script**ure! Every person in customer service uses scripts whether they learned them from a sheet of paper or copied what other people said. Don't tell me you don't like to use scripts because trust me - you are scripted.

When we first opened our BDC, both the sales teams and my staff took an equal share of inbound calls. Each of the calls was recorded, and the managers of each sales staff were required to listen to their team calls daily so they could provide coaching. The old "inspect what you expect" philosophy was to be followed. Since my role was the administrator overseeing calls and all activities, my job was to provide the reports showing which salespeople were and were not using the scripts. We also evaluated if the managers were listening to their calls. As a result, our company president pulled all telephone calls from the sales departments and gave them exclusively to the BDC.

Things were moving along well in my department. It brought me great pleasure to lead a team of professionals who enjoyed their work and made my job easier. I learned a lot about team building, interdepartmental communications, and technology during my time in the BDC. It would have been great if my calling and my purpose in launching new things and developing new staff members had been understood. Maybe it would have been clear why after only a few months when things were clicking along smoothly, the boredom set in. It was time for another change, but I didn't see it coming.

MILE MARKER

Practice and perfect your strategies for success. Take ideas others have created, and you make them your own. Refine who you are to maximize your new skills and resources.

THIRTY-ONE

MILE THIRTY – KNOW THE WHY OF YOUR PROJECTS

IT'S SOMEWHAT surprising that my tenure with Mitsubishi lasted as long as it did. Since late 2001, I've served full-time or contracting with Mitsubishi for all but two years. After all, this entrepreneurial mindset doesn't allow me to be content in one place for very long. At the writing of this book, I'm coming off a ten-year streak of full-time employment as a performance manager and trainer for Mitsubishi Motors North America.

After leaving Saturn of Orange County, there were a few other companies before taking the job as sales operations specialist for Mitsubishi, whose headquarters was in Cypress, California. It was a beautiful, 45-minute drive to their office from home. Talk radio was prominent during the two years, making the trek back and forth to the North American campus enjoyable.

I remember the first time I met Jim Vitz. It was the day

of my interview at headquarters. Jim was a high-energy, "efficiency madman" who I grew to love as a leader and person. If you had passion and enthusiasm for what you were doing, and if you were able to explain why you were doing it, Jim gave you every ounce of support you needed to succeed. Others weren't as fond of his approach. Some were afraid of him.

At the start of every meeting to which Jim was invited, the first words out of his mouth the instant he rushed into the room (yes, rushed!) was, "Why are we here?" There had to be a reason for the meeting and some value behind it or, in Jim's mind, it was a waste of time. You'll get no disagreement from me! Far too many meetings occur simply because of tradition or formality, and nothing gets done. Jim taught me clarity of vision was a critical factor to efficiency and success. Every training piece and every memo needed to begin with a purpose. My training courses are still built the same way today.

Several years later, Sinek would write the now-famous book, *Start with Why! How Great Leaders Inspire Everyone to Take Action*. While some didn't feel inspired to take action from Jim's leadership, they all ensured they followed his strategy of leading with "why." Jim led the way long before the idea of "why" was in vogue.

MILE MARKER

Know exactly why you do each task you do. Have a clear vision and purpose for every plan you put in place. Every meeting you set must have a reason, even if it's just planning to have fun.

THIRTY-TWO

MILE THIRTY-ONE – NOT ALL EXPERTS KNOW "YOUR" STUFF

ONE OF THE significant projects my department participated in during my first stint with Mitsubishi was a series of videos focused on improving customer satisfaction. The project cost was somewhere around $2 million, and the vendor contracted to develop the video scripts was JD Power and Associates.

The project manager, team leader, and lead writer were all terrific people. Each one held master's degrees or higher, and they approached the project with professionalism and efficiency. But none of them had a clue about what happens with salespeople and customers in retail automotive. A lack of real-world experience isn't at all uncommon. Most outside vendors have never worked in a retail environment, so all of their knowledge is theoretical.

My task in the project was to review the drafts of each script and provide notes or edits. As it turned out, the script reviews lasted anywhere from four to six hours each. It wasn't as if the writing was poor. These writers were experienced and educated in their craft. But the terminology, phrases, and examples given weren't realistic to what salespeople say, or what customers experienced at each step of the buying process. We all were, quite frankly, a bit shocked at how little a company like JD Power and Associates knew about the sales process in an industry they held so much influence over.

The result of the project was a success. After the videos rolled out, coupled with other training and exams via the Mitsubishi Academy, the brand's SSI score rose 32 points year-over-year, and everyone was happy with our team. But the experience, and the amount our department paid out, caused Jim and others to reconsider the value provided by JD Power and Associates. Jim created a new tagline for them; I will never forget it. He called them, "The Great Pretenders." A few years later, JD Power and Associates were sold to McGraw Hill Financial and continue to be a primary source of rating customer experiences.

MILE MARKER

Leverage your expertise and the expertise of others. Make sure the people in charge of projects are the most knowledgeable and most qualified regardless of their degree or their reputed level of knowledge.

THIRTY-THREE

MILE THIRTY-ONE – BE READY TO PIVOT

AS TIME WENT ON, a new opportunity came my way to oversee and coach others as trainers, and to host sales product and process training videos. One of those videos included the US launch of the Mitsubishi Lancer Evolution. My opportunity to learn to drive the Evo at Danny McKeever's Fast Lane Racing School in Willow Springs, California, will never be forgotten. There are still old VHS tapes of the EVO customer maintenance video tucked away in Mitsubishi dealerships. Managers bring them out to show from time to time—what a great experience.

Soon afterward, an event on the home front required me to pivot once more. It required I work from home, and we began the first trek into an automotive training company. The original name was DelRae Consulting and Development which we began in California. DelRae Learning and Development is the renamed company we now own and operate out of Arizona.

Working from home has its positives and negatives. It certainly gives us an advantage now that Covid-19 has impacted the world and reduced travel to a crawl. The fortunate thing is the relationships established during my work with Mitsubishi and their network of vendors gave me a foothold to begin working remotely right out of the gate.

Another illustration of being ready to pivot came during the Fixed Ops Roundtable event in June of 2020. As discussed in other places, technology isn't always perfect. Neither are human beings. When you have forty-plus presenters joining an event virtually from all over the country, you should anticipate a few hiccups. We did, and we were ready.

I've seen Arnold Schwarzenegger quoted quite a lot on the topic of having a backup plan. He says, "Forget plan B. To test yourself and grow, you have to operate without a safety net." I suppose that depends on whether you're risking your own life or the lives of others. Karl Wallenda died on live TV falling from a tightrope. But he knew the risk. When we do a broadcast where others expect us to deliver, a backup plan is important.

During one particular segment, a guest's entire Wi-Fi crashed, and they were unable to join us on time. But having prepared a discussion to jump to in case of a technical challenge made us look good. The pivot went seamlessly, and the show continued without any evidence of a problem.

MILE MARKER

Be prepared when things don't go as planned. Expect the unexpected. Make alternate or backup plans and be ready to implement them at a moment's notice.

THIRTY-FOUR

MILE THIRTY-TWO – BELIEVE IN YOUR ABILITIES

BEFORE LEAVING MITSUBISHI IN 2003, I was introduced to Ted Ings, one of the vendors supplying training solutions for fixed operations. For anyone who doesn't know, fixed operations represent the service side of a dealership's business. Manufacturers call it aftersales. Ted's company, Auto University, provided training for service advisors and managers on customer contact and selling skills. Ted is a man of action. He doesn't hold back when he decides to do something, and he doesn't hold back from new endeavors. If I've learned one thing from Ted, it's to be fearless and willing to say yes to any adventure.

One of my first responsibilities in working with Ted was to observe his classes and refine the material to align with Mitsubishi's processes. Ted is one of those business pioneers who often finds himself on the cutting edge of the automotive industry. Along with my friend Shawn Ryder, Ted ran one of the first automotive e-learning platforms. Ted has continued to launch new strategies, including the highly successful Fixed Ops Roundtable® events, which are attended by hundreds of automotive leaders from all over the world.

After leaving Mitsubishi, our new business contracted with Ted, where I served as "Dean of Development" for AutoUniversity.com. The site provided subscription training services, a newsletter, featured articles, and a video e-mail called "The Tip of the Day." Many of the strategies we worked on at the time are still being utilized in the industry today. Ted still presents "The Tip of the Day" from his new company, Center for Performance Improvement® Automotive.

Working from a home office in my garage, we had a makeshift video studio with a green screen, video camera, lighting, ear prompter, editing software, and a fancy desk. My primary role was to produce content for the website and other training resources, though I was not the sole provider of ideas and influence. Ted had other partnerships and trainers who contributed mightily to the content as subject matter experts.

While AutoUniversity.com was a success, it was the in-dealership element of the business model that caused Mitsubishi to connect with Ted in the first place. It was the same element that opened a door for business with Mazda North American Operations. While our operation was small compared to some big training companies like Sandy (Now GP Strategies), Maritz, or Jackson–Dawson, we had confidence in our ability to deliver a world-class product.

Since Ted was located in New Jersey and my home was in Southern California, it made sense for me and one of the in-dealership trainers, Jack, to make the presentation to Mazda, which was and still is located in Irvine, California.

It was a gorgeous day when I met Jack in the parking lot at Mazda. We soon were escorted upstairs to meet the project team. Jack explained the in-dealership element, while my idea of training the process from the customer's perspective turned out to be a hit as well. A few days later, we got the call letting us know our group would be developing and training Mazda's Professional Selling Skills for the Full Circle Service Process.

As the project launched, and we began asking questions, we learned the visionary behind the project was in Hiroshima, Japan, at Mazda's worldwide headquarters. After asking how we could best understand the vision, one of the project managers said, "The best thing you could do is go to Japan!" I called Ted up after the meeting, and without hesitation, he said, "Okay, let's go to Japan!"

As previously mentioned, one of the biggest misconceptions people have about life on the road is that we who travel for work enjoy a life of luxury, leisure, and an abundance of site seeing. While there may be a few folks who can extend their business trips into mini vacations, it has rarely been the case with me.

Unless my wife comes along, and we have planned specific time before or after a trip, it's getting off the plane, grab some food, work from the hotel, iron the clothes (wash-rinse-repeat), until the week is over and it's time to get on the plane headed home. And while we were fortunate enough to bring family members to Japan with us, my and Ted's time was all business the entire trip.

The project itself turned out great. The training we delivered both in the classroom and in the dealerships was very well received. The accolades were coming in for the entire team, and business started booming. We even had a special training event just for our company with the great Brian Tracy.

It was a fantastic time. But as you may have noticed, life doesn't always remain peaches and cream. Less than a year after launching the project, Ted and I parted ways, if only temporarily.

MILE MARKER

Ensure you are trained in the necessary skills, and that you practice those skills, and you perform at a high level. Work hard to become confident in your abilities. You are then the expert, and you can show it every time to everyone.

THIRTY-FIVE

MILE THIRTY-THREE – AVOID BURNING BRIDGES

ONE OF THE more important lessons anyone can learn in business, or when working for someone else, is to leave on good terms. Oh sure, there are often reasons to be unhappy, but there is wisdom in a saying that came my way many years earlier: "Is this the hill on which you care to die?" Is it worth burning a bridge with you on it, and to never have the opportunity to cross the bridge again?

As you've already seen, I have repeatedly returned to employers and business relationships. Now I was being asked to return to the Saturn training team. Others who have worked for or with the same companies left on not so good terms. As a result, their opportunities for returning were permanently closed.

It was a different time for Saturn. They had almost been cut from the General Motors lineup at the same time Oldsmobile had been eliminated. But someone was smart enough to ask existing Saturn owners what other brands of General Motors vehicles they would consider buying were Saturn to go away. Their answer stunned many at GM. Almost 2,000,000 people surveyed said they would return to an import brand rather than purchase any other General Motors vehicle. Instead of cutting the brand, considerable investment was made to improve the Saturn product.

One of the things we used to say in retail was, "Everybody makes a pretty good car these days, so you're not going to end up with a poorly built vehicle." Products built by Saturn in their first ten years of existence fell into this category. General Motors, however, didn't invest much money in Saturn or product development. The platform changed very little except for an exterior redesign for 1996. It was the same car skinned three different ways.

When I returned as a contract trainer, Saturn had invested a lot of money in producing new designs. These cars would win awards, and they would quickly cause jealousy among other General Motors brands, namely Chevrolet. The year after Saturn's Aura sedan won the award for North American Car of the Year, Chevrolet demanded they rebadge the same vehicle as a Malibu. They did, and it would win the same prize for Chevy the following year.

For the first time in Saturn's history, it shared a platform with another GM nameplate, and it spelled the beginning of the end. Another decision, giving former Oldsmobile dealers new Saturn franchises, set Saturn on a course creating even more division. It made training these folks more difficult because they had no intention of doing business The Saturn Way. As each successive year passed, Saturn became more like other GM brands, and less like the leader in customer satisfaction they'd been ten years earlier.

As Saturn started investing in a new vehicle lineup, it

upgraded its facilities and updated its sales processes. Customers had begun doing more research online, and changes in retail experiences were also expected. Once again, I was asked to be the lead trainer for the new process. It was a lot of work, and it involved many unique activities, including trips to shopping malls to visit cutting-edge retail stores like the Apple Store, Williams Sonoma, and LUSH. If they were providing an exceptional customer experience, we visited and integrated what we learned into the new Saturn consultative sales process.

In the next two years, we were busy. As the lead trainer, I traveled a lot to a variety of areas in the country to pilot the new processes. During one particular week, I had to train in Texas on a Monday and Tuesday, then catch a plane Tuesday night for a five-hour flight to Northern Michigan, where another pilot training was to occur on Wednesday morning. Not only was it a long day, but I was sick. Still, the program turned out very good, and I learned a great deal about project management.

MILE MARKER

Build and maintain excellent relationships, both personally and professionally. Great relationships allow you to return and do business with past connections because you left on a positive note.

THIRTY-SIX

MILE THIRTY-FOUR – DIVERSIFICATION VS. LOYALTY

DURING THE SUMMER OF 2008, JD Power and Associates reached out with a request for me to participate in a three-month project. Wisdom dictates contractors should avoid putting all their eggs in one basket. At the time, all my eggs were in General Motors basket. My agreement with the contract company allowed for cancellation of schedules for either party within 60 days prior. Sixty days was plenty of time to prepare for the project with JD Power and Associates.

But General Motors wasn't happy. The Saturn project was significant, and they didn't want me to leave for three months in the middle of summer. They pleaded with me to stay and made me feel bad by telling me how much work they'd given me over the past few years instead of other people. I caved and declined the offer from JD Power.

As it turns out, not taking the job with JD Power and

Associates was a business mistake. As a Christian, and someone who takes the Bible seriously, it makes sense to trust in the scripture which says, "God causes all things to work for good for those who love him and are called according to his purposes."

In other words, don't look back with regret. My approach, instead, is to view it as a learning experience. My hope is this will guide my future decisions. But what happened several months later devastated my family and me financially: The day before receiving $17 billion in bailout money from Uncle Sam, the General Motors project manager called me and canceled all my future work as GM filed for bankruptcy.

MILE MARKER

Be wise about managing your business relationships. You can be both loyal and calculated concerning plans and associations.

THIRTY-SEVEN

MILE THIRTY-FIVE – FACE HARD TIMES HEAD ON

THERE HAVE BEEN difficult times in my life, personally and professionally. Some of those stories are for another time. This book is focused on my professional life. The recession of 2008 halted everything, and our lives were significantly impacted. The value of our home plummeted. The strategies to help consumers refinance their homes didn't work as efficiently as one might anticipate. And very few companies were hiring automotive trainers.

One company that did look promising was AutoNation. My good friend from Saturn, Charlie Brown, had been working with them for quite a while, and he referred me to the president of the South Orange County area for Auto-Nation. The interview process was long and intense, but after the third and final interview, an offer was made, and I accepted. AutoNation was the opportunity we hoped was going to save our home and inevitable bankruptcy. I was excited. Then the unexpected happened.

At the time, AutoNation had a policy requiring qualified internal candidates to be first in line for jobs with which they applied. After we had agreed to terms, and a start date was set, I received a call from the regional president informing me one of their general managers had decided to apply for the trainer position. And since it was company policy, they had no choice but to give him the job. The news was devastating.

As I searched for work, opportunities were few and far between. Then I came across an ad for Southwest Airlines. The new job was an opportunity to work in customer service at their Phoenix location with full benefits and a decent wage. Southwest Airlines has been, and still is, one of the better companies to work for with a fun environment and advancement opportunities. I was reintroduced to the FISH! Philosophy®, as they embraced all the elements of Play, Make Their Day, Be There, and Choose Your Attitude. Not everything was rosy, but it was an excellent company for which to work. Plus, I flew for free, and free flights were necessary because, at the time, we still lived in Southern California.

For me to work at Southwest Airlines, the arrangement required me to live with my in-laws during the week and fly home on the weekends. Given we already knew the life of a traveler, being away from home during the week was not unusual. And after six months, Southwest allowed us to work a flex schedule and advance to a supervisor position.

What happened next put me to the test physically and mentally, but it was another opportunity to see how far one could take this thing called life. Remember, about nine months earlier, my income ceased, and I went for several months earning nothing. Now at Southwest, my wages were less than $15 an hour, but the benefits were great, and there was free air travel for my wife and parents. Still, if we had hopes of saving our home, something needed to change.

Then a call came from a training partner of General Motors. Saturn was shutting down, and to retain as many Saturn customers as possible, Chevrolet service departments would need to learn how to treat customers in a way that would make the Saturn owners happy. So, they called me.

For the next eight months, my schedule was to work Friday evening through Sunday night doing double shifts for Southwest airlines, and sleep in the back of a Saturn station wagon between shifts. Then Monday through Thursday, I traveled to Chevrolet stores in the Western US, teaching them how to treat Saturn customers in a way a customer should be treated. It sounds ridiculous, doesn't it? It was ironic the very GM brand most responsible for Saturn's demise was now getting the benefit of Saturn's customers coming to their service departments. Life, huh?

You might wonder why I continued to work for Southwest Airlines after getting the training gig with GM. First, I needed the benefits for my family. Second, the assignment with GM was temporary. It was only going to last nine months to a year, and then nobody knew what else might open up. The economy was still in trouble, and the automotive industry wasn't recovering very well. There was hope a training role at the airline would open up, and I could get out of automotive once and for all.

I love some aspects of the car business. I love the people, but the policies, strategies, and processes being employed at the manufacturer and dealer level were – and sadly still are – one step ahead of a stone age mentality.

After seven months of doing double duty, a call came from my good friend Bob Johnson at Mitsubishi Motors. He told me of an opportunity in their Western Zone for a retail performance manager. The job would include travel, but it would provide a much better income and return all the benefits from my original hire date nine years earlier. I would get to work with people I'd known for decades, and I'd get to be part of rebuilding a brand that had nearly left the US just a few years earlier. Here again was an opportunity to work with a company I'd left earlier, but in good standing.

MILE MARKER

Don't run from trouble. When difficult situations arise, face them straight up. One way or another, you know there will be painful situations, and running from them will only delay the outcome and make it worse.

THIRTY-EIGHT

MILE THIRTY-SIX – IT'S OKAY TO TAKE CARE OF YOUR FAMILY

WHEN THE CALL came from Mitsubishi, my emotions were mixed. I was certainly grateful for the opportunity, but the work with the folks at Southwest Airlines was great. What settled the matter was learning my advancement to the position of a trainer at Southwest Airlines was declined, and it did not mean a significant income increase had it been approved.

While there's more to work than money, my experience and expertise as a trainer were undoubtedly worth more than a few dollars an hour. Plus, I had great relationships with the people at Mitsubishi. Like all OEMs, the "working folks" are hard workers, most have ethical standards, and they are genuinely passionate about the brand they represent. I've developed amazing friendships while working at Mitsubishi. They are some of the best people in the world.

Mitsubishi takes care of its employees from a policy and

human resources standpoint. They provide exceptional benefits. They are fair when it comes to needing personal time off for family or health matters. And the corporation went to the aid of those distressed when national and global crises occur. When, for example, our Mitsubishi Motors North America (MMNA) family in Puerto Rico suffered greatly from Hurricane Maria, the company and the employees stepped up in a big way to support our team. I have nothing but praise for how Mitsubishi has taken care of me financially. Upon my return in 2010, there was every intention of finishing my professional career with Mitsubishi.

It's also important to consider your family. While being an entrepreneur is a calling, there's a scripture that says, "He who doesn't care for the needs of his own house is worse than an unbeliever." I did everything possible to earn enough money to provide for the needs of my family. I've made mistakes along the way, and my life is still a work in progress. While many "influencers" promote living your dreams at all costs, my philosophy is somewhat different. It's okay to set your goals aside to care for your family if need be. There should be a way to do both. Having a consistent, stable income and health insurance can bring a feeling of peace and security for a season.

MILE MARKER

Choose to put the needs of others ahead of your dreams when necessary. Sometimes, meeting your family's needs is the best thing you can do for yourself in the short-term and long-term. Look for ways to fulfill your dreams while not negatively impacting the ones you love most.

THIRTY-NINE

MILE THIRTY – SEVEN – YOUR PLANS WON'T ALWAYS WORK OUT

THE NEW ROLE at MMNA was Retail Performance Manager (RPM) for the west zone. There were only two zones at the time—an east and a west, with one RPM for each zone. My friend and colleague, Andrew Schultz, held down the east zone. The job description for this position identified areas where my retail experience and skills as a trainer should have been maximized. When the job title of RPM was created, there were good intentions. Being an RPM was a pretty high position within the corporate structure.

To meet the training needs of 300 dealers, it would require the field team to deliver at least some of the training during their visits. As a result, most of the RPM's time should have been spent developing the Area Sales Managers (ASM), who would then coach their district teams on new training and in-dealership initiatives. The other elements of the job included monthly webinars, curriculum development when needed for the national office, delivering quarterly training in top 20 markets, and special events like ride-and-drives.

Unfortunately, the ASM position had developed into another layer for commercial activities and oversight. ASMs were not available to be trained, and the rest of the field team were either delivering programs, pushing wholesale, or firefighting for their dealers, the zone, the national office, or all three. Ideally, the field team should be helping their dealerships produce more retail sales. As a result, wholesale would take care of itself as dealers would need to purchase more inventory by default. But they weren't allowed to focus on those activities. Training has always been considered less of a priority than keeping the factory busy (though if you do training right, the factory will stay active). Things have only gotten worse since then.

There were many times I rejected offers to be either a district manager, an ASM, and even a zone sales manager. Why endure the brain damage of being yelled at for things beyond my control? At least the RPM position was somewhat autonomous. Being an automotive district manager has become a thankless job, one can compare to yelling at a tree and expecting it to grow fruit. But when the farmer's water supply and fertilizer are cut off, there is no way the fruit will grow.

My thinking is if you focus on what makes a tree healthy and vibrant, the fruit will take care of itself. Fruit doesn't magically grow because you tell it to and discounting the price of unripe fruit won't make it taste better. Of course, my skills have never led me to become the key decision-maker at an automotive manufacturer, so who am I to judge their decisions? Then again, one doesn't need to take poison to know it kills.

The main priority for my job during the first five years was to develop and deliver in-dealer training by request, provide quarterly training at the zone office for the field team, and deliver special training events in our top 20 markets at the request of the national office. The job itself was great. Participants loved the training. It just wasn't very efficient or effective.

Trying to train 150 dealerships with one trainer spread out across half the United States was not realistic. Financially, this was a good job. But my attitude has always been to get better and improve things at my company. There's nothing more frustrating than to be on the front lines, see what is needed, and have your superiors ignore what you have to say. Businesses will never improve when leadership refuses to listen to their team members. Eventually, the good ideas will stop because people feel like they're wasting their breath.

MILE MARKER

Sink your roots in deep through sharpening your skills and developing yourself as a person. When the winds of change are powerful, or when a flood comes, you're able to withstand because you're prepared.

FORTY

MILE THIRTY-EIGHT – COVER YOUR ASSETS (CYA)

ANOTHER THING common in big corporations is to hunt for reasons things aren't going well and to find people to blame. This is especially true if your position functions with very little oversight. When you work for others or for yourself it's important to follow a process of stellar ethics and respect for policies and procedures. Fortunately for me, my methods have always included keeping track of my actions, emails, and every place I visited on every day. My expense reports have always been tight, and within company guidelines. Having worked for a number of large companies, I've made sure my communications, reports, and schedule were buttoned up, never wanting to leave a door open that could call my actions into question.

The following two experiences aren't unique to me, but they provide insight into how messed up things can get within large corporations. One such situation occurred when a group of key leaders within my organization met together to review underperforming dealers. As each dealership was discussed, the people responsible for oversight would be required to explain.

In one case, a request had been made for me to provide training at an underperforming dealership. Our known training process was to accept any request if an opening in my schedule permitted. That said, a call needed to be made to both the district manager and the area manager to ensure the dealership would be ready for training. In other words, it wasn't my decision at all.

At the time of the request, both managers told me the dealership in question wasn't in a place to be trained any time soon. My schedule and my priorities for several months had been predetermined in a conference call a few weeks prior. Everyone knew this. But when asked by the president of the company I worked for why a particular dealership was still not improving, the response from the person who had asked me to train them was, "I've asked Gene to do training there, but he always says he's too busy." Did someone get the number of that bus?

Evidently the president asked each of my superiors if they knew what my schedule was, and each one said no. But a simple call to one of our administrators would have resulted in a quick answer about my schedule, as it was posted on our interoffice Outlook calendar and had been for eight months prior. Sometimes even the highest levels of leadership are not prepared to be called out, and they panicked. Since I wasn't in the room, I was an easy scapegoat.

Here's a message to anyone in leadership: When a corporate culture is based on fear and not trust, you will find many bus drivers in the company who are willing to run others over to save their own skin. It's a problem for many prominent companies. While it was wrong to throw me under the bus, it was the company's culture that created the environment that made it possible.

The next experience I had was related to expense reports. After a change in leadership at the top of my organization, an analysis was done of everyone's expenses. That's not a bad thing. In this case, certain expense categories came under scrutiny, and several team members were called out. The first area of concern was related to the administration's oversight and approval process. Individual field team members had taken some liberties concerning expenses, and several people were fired. For the next six months, every expense report was subject to audit. Because I followed policy to the letter, my expenses were not a concern. It felt great to know that while others were running scared, I didn't have the slightest concern. In a way, it was a lot like paying taxes. If you don't cheat, you don't have to worry about an audit. Minor mistakes are acceptable and understood. But those are easily rectified.

MILE MARKER

Make sure to track your actions and activities. Be able to give an honest account whenever someone asks you. Doing so will validate you as someone who can be trusted.

FORTY-ONE

MILE THIRTY–NINE – INTEGRITY IS THE BEST OPTION

DURING THE LAST few years with Mitsubishi, a new department called The Customer Experience (CX) department was formed, and a new director was assigned. I was fortunate enough to work with John Nakamoto, Bob Johnson, Kiri Kiely-Rodriguez, and David Walker. They, along with many others at Mitsubishi Motors North America, are terrific team members and great friends.

My title changed from RPM to National Sales Trainer, and we eventually stopped doing quarterly training events. We focused almost exclusively on new dealerships and underperforming SSI dealers. We also added a service drive training element to new dealer training. Service training had been missing from the platform for nearly a decade. Returning to my fixed operations roots was a positive thing. During the last six months with the company, my job included supporting the launch and development of a new tablet tool for dealerships called MiShowroom and MiDelivery.

In April 2019, we were told Mitsubishi would be moving their long-time headquarters from Cypress, California, to Franklin, Tennessee. My position with Mitsubishi would also be eliminated in December of the same year. It didn't come as a complete shock, but there would be some work to prepare for my next adventure. The first step for me involved returning to social media, namely, LinkedIn. It opened up a world of new connections and opportunities I'd never thought would unfold the way.

During the transition away from being a full-time employee, my strategy was to make sure 100% of my working hours were given to Mitsubishi Motors. Ethics and integrity are crucial. Exploring future opportunities would happen on my own time. There have been numerous instances when outside companies asked me to write content for the automotive industry while still employed by Mitsubishi. It wasn't an article or something simple. It was training content. I always refused because it would have been a conflict of interest.

Some people are okay with doing side hustles within their industry because, quite frankly, nobody would know. But there's only one person I have to answer to, and it's me. More importantly, I answer to God. The apostle James said, "Whoever knows the right thing to do and fails to do it, for them it is a sin." (By the way, sin just means to miss the mark.)

Occasionally the lines become blurred. There was one instance in my career where there was a choice between the external client and the internal client who contracted me to do a job. Both were my clients. I had been brought in to replace another project manager, and one of the partners overseeing IT from outside the country got impatient with the client. He didn't want to make any more changes without charging them, and he wanted me to tell the customer.

I felt this was wrong because he knew the problems created by the previous rep, and the client happened to be a major automotive player. I took up the external client's position and withheld specific details from the IT partner to keep the job moving. We finally got it done. When we reviewed what had happened, my contract was canceled, and I learned a lesson. I should have let the local partner know of the conflict and kept my personal opinions out of it.

I've done my best to carry integrity into my work inside and outside of the corporate world. I've been asked to do things at every level of employment that I wasn't comfortable with. Saying no is a lot safer than you might think. It may feel like there is pressure from the top to "trick the system" and go along with the request, but when you say no, your superior is then put on the spot and held accountable. I've had a few who said, "It's not an ethical problem," to which I say, "Okay. I just want it to be on record that I don't agree." And I will follow that up with a written communication. Has that rubbed people wrong? Yes. But I've always slept well at night when I've held my integrity.

Doing the right thing always pays off. Though my full-time position with Mitsubishi was eliminated, I was respected enough that they hired me as a contractor to continue providing training after my employment ended.

MILE MARKER

Practice an ethical standard, whether others do or not. It doesn't matter if no one will find out because your integrity is at stake, and you'll sleep well because you're doing the right thing.

FORTY-TWO

MILE FORTY – BE A FARMER, NOT A FRUIT PICKER

RATHER THAN BEGIN TRAINING at Mitsubishi dealerships in January 2020 as initially planned, the first dealership visits took place in March, just before Covid-19 shut everyone down. What appeared to be a profitable relationship was put on indefinite hold. Since most dealerships were closed to everything except maintenance and repairs, it was determined the training offered by my company would have to be put on hold as well. Some objected to providing the training remotely, and the crushing blow to sales eliminated the training budget.

During the transition from April 2019, I started reading business books and exploring new strategies for success. One of those books was written by a former Cal State MBA professor named Chris Haroun. In his book, *101 Things They Don't Teach You in Business School*, Haroun suggested anyone looking for a job should get themselves on

LinkedIn. Joining LinkedIn has turned out to be one of the better recommendations I've received.

Through LinkedIn, my followers have reached nearly 7,000. Having less than 10,000 followers is a relatively small number for almost a year on the platform. The "influencers" will post something like, "If you want to grow your network, like this post and connect with everyone else who does the same." But my intention has never been to make connections and grow followers just to do it. My reasoning has been to establish my credentials and make business connections. Despite the view of some who think it doesn't work, LinkedIn has been more than worthwhile.

At the time of this writing, I haven't made a lot of money as a direct result of clients found on LinkedIn. But the connections and relationships I've made have put me in a position to launch our company into highly profitable territory. It's the old farmer vs. fruit-picker mentality. Training is a lot like farming.

A farmer will buy a field, plow the ground, nurture the soil, plant the seeds, water the earth, and ensure the environment for growth is optimal. But the plant doesn't produce fruit until the proper season. I'm much more of a farmer than I am a fruit picker. I'm not interested in trying to pull the fruit off a tree if it isn't ripe. In automotive sales, however, they do this all the time. They add "incentives," which act like ripening agents to entice customers to "buy now." They don't think about the fact that all they're doing is pulling the fruit off the tree early. It will never result in more fruit, and it often damages the tree and the farm in the long term.

Additionally, I had time to write this book, with another one due in a few months. Sitting around and pouting about the bad crop or harvest is never a good use of time or emotional energy. Farmers don't lament the weather for long. They mend fences, they repair their equipment, and they get educated on new strategies. They start over. Farmers start over EVERY YEAR!

MILE MARKER

Only pick the fruit when it's ripe because the long-term impact on the tree and your business by pulling the fruit off too soon is destructive. Run your business and establish your relationships with the big picture in mind. Adapt and be agile, but don't change good fundamentals when economic factors change.

FORTY-THREE

MILE FORTY–ONE – CONTENT IS KING

ONE OF THE first connections I made on LinkedIn was with Ted Ings, who I wrote about previously. He told me how he'd found success on the LinkedIn platform after returning to automotive from a brief stint in healthcare. Many of his connections became my connections. And while my ultimate goal had been to expand my territory outside of automotive, the adage "once you're in the car business you never get out of it" has undoubtedly been part of my story.

Balancing who I am as a person, what I have to offer others, and my expertise and experiences in automotive have been learning experiences. I could have a more significant following on social media if I focused more on family stories, personal life, and general topics. That would also be true if more time was spent on platforms like Facebook or Twitter. I suspect it would interest more people. My content now focuses primarily on automotive and business strategies for success and personal development, philosophy, and wisdom.

Being a creative type, I've found producing content to be somewhat comfortable. I've done articles, videos, text posts, comic strips, and more. All of them are effective. It doesn't matter how old you are, how you look, or what your budget is. If your content is interesting and valuable, people will engage with it. If you're interested in a big following, it's not hard. Go to Facebook, Twitter, or Instagram, and just post anything and engage with everyone. That's not for me. Maybe one day, when our business is more established, and we have someone whose sole job is to manage our social media accounts, you may see us there.

The same is true when it comes to developing training and education material. The stories have to be good. There is an adage that says, "facts tell, and stories sell." I'm sure it's true. I need to work on that more myself because so much of what I do requires research. The information has to be accurate, so the natural tendency is to build training around facts. Get creative with your facts and make them attractive. Turn the data into a story, if possible.

MILE MARKER

Ensure your stories bring value to customers and potential customers. Give away advice for free because it builds confidence and trust in you as an advisor, trainer, or consultant. Make your business a beacon of light in your industry.

FORTY-FOUR

MILE FORTY-ONE – BE CONSISTENT AND AUTHENTIC

ANOTHER THING I learned about being on LinkedIn is that many people who may never comment or like a post are still watching. Many of them are significant business leaders and entrepreneurs. Some "lurkers" are even accomplished authors like John Christensen, who co-authored the book FISH! Based on the world's famous Pike Place Fish Market, the book has sold more than 6-million copies, and it launched a training phenomenon that has influenced companies like Southwest Airlines, Zappos, Microsoft, and many more.

I have experienced the benefits of the FISH! Philosophy® at both Saturn and Southwest Airlines. When I saw Charthouse Learning on LinkedIn, I quickly connected to those in the company. I also connected with John Christensen, but I had no contact with him for several months. I don't even recall him engaging in any of my content. But he was watching.

The first announcement I saw about a Train-The-Trainer (T-3) session for FISH! was in July 2019, and it was set for October. These sessions were designed for internal corporate trainers or HR representatives to take the training back to train their team members. I contacted the folks at Charthouse Learning (home of the FISH! Philosophy®) and asked if they were offering a T-3 session for contract trainers who could support the FISH! Philosophy® as affiliates, or as additional members of their training team. At the time, they had no plans for such a strategy.

A few months later, I hit them up again. They responded kindly and let me know they were thinking about it, but at this time, there were no plans for taking the training outside the scope of their current process. But persistence pays off, as does posting content consistent with a philosophy you say you want to support and promote.

One afternoon in mid-December, I received a call from someone in Minnesota. As with any number I'm unfamiliar with, I let it go to voicemail. As I played the message, a smile broke out on my face. "Hi, this is John Christensen, co-author of FISH! I know you've been in contact with us, and I've been following your content on LinkedIn." I enjoyed hearing the voicemail. It was an indication of the effort I'd made to produce valuable content was paying off. And this was just the beginning.

On a side note, it's vital to notice the similarity between how my role at Saturn advanced, and how my association with Charthouse Learning has evolved. Both began with a desire to become something or someone. Next, there was a specific plan and a connection to the people who would help me achieve the goal. Finally, a key player within the organization contacted me based on my persistence and consistent behavior. Therein lay a pivotal secret to success.

Since December 2019, I've had no fewer than six additional business leaders contact me, letting me know they've been following my content on LinkedIn. One of them resulted in connection with strong potential for growth. Organic growth is the result of being authentic on social media. What you appear to be online should match the real you when a face-to-face meeting occurs or connected via Zoom or telephone.

MILE MARKER

Social messaging must align with who you are offline. Be authentic, so when people meet you in person, you're the same person they see virtually.

FORTY-FIVE

MILE FORTY–TWO – LEAVE A LEGACY

WHEN THE ANNOUNCEMENT came from Mitsubishi in April 2019 that my full-time employment would end the following December, we decided to reopen our training company. The previous company was called DelRae Consulting and Development. We changed the name because our focus was going to be more on the educational aspect rather than the consulting aspect for businesses and individuals. Additionally, the idea behind this new company would be to extend the scope beyond just the automotive world and leave a legacy that would involve our family if desired.

We're highly motivated by the proverb that says, "A good person leaves an inheritance to his/her children's children." Neither my wife's parents nor my parents will be leaving us anything substantial financially. I'm not saying our parents haven't left us a valuable legacy. But the scripture I mentioned is clearly about money. And we want to bless our family with something substantial, so they will have the freedom to pursue their gifts without needing to rely on the government or be stressed out by needing to provide for the basics of food, clothing, and shelter.

Another thing happened while crafting this book was the realization that DelRae Learning is just an entity but not a company. It's a place to funnel business legally, and it establishes a platform for credibility. We have a lot of work to do to create a clear vision and purpose for what this company will become because my wife and I eventually want to work at, and for, our business together.

Regardless of how successful our company becomes we have no intention of leaving a fortune to our kids. An inheritance, yes. The wealth they'll have to earn on their own. We still have a lot to do ourselves. We have taken care of the basics like a living will and family trust. We'll leave a share of whatever we earn to charity, and we will be faithful stewards of the gifts we've received from God's Grace.

At the time of this writing, my primary focus is automotive learning and development because my experience requires it, and there are no other employees except me. My wife, a registered nurse, has previously been trained in biological warfare response strategies. She's been an instructor for the Red Cross, to county paramedics, and at her hospital. She was the co-director of junior high ministries with me. She is currently getting her master's degree in nursing, and she'll be a great educator shortly.

Each of our four children has taught, coached, or provided training to others. Some have done it in business, some as athletic trainers and coaches, and some have done it online. It makes sense to move our company in a direction where each of our children and their families can be involved should they so choose. We would love that, and they all have a great deal to offer.

MILE MARKER

Have a clear plan for what you will leave behind. Establish your legacy. Your family and future generations will be blessed because of your work and life.

FORTY-SIX

MILE FORTY-THREE – DEFINE YOUR TARGET AUDIENCE

One of the biggest challenges when beginning any business is defining your target audience. When I first returned to social media (and in particular LinkedIn), my content followed a shotgun approach. I wanted to move my focus outside automotive and more toward general business learning and development.

Given the ultimate goal we have for our company, it makes sense that my mind was leaning in a direction away from the car business. But it didn't help me establish any clients, and I've since learned to focus more on improving a specific group of people who have a particular need to be addressed.

One of my connections on LinkedIn, Monty Clark, painted the picture of a camel coming upon a man who is all alone wandering through the desert. While he may have several needs, his real issue is what Monte calls a water problem. He also shared with me that, "A confused mind always says 'no!'"

I'm still having trouble nailing down precisely what problems I want to solve because I have several skills and many things I enjoy doing. Ben Franklin is famous for saying, "Be a jack of all trades and a master of one" (not none). My passion is for creativity, but my knowledge is in automotive.

I changed everything on my social media to reflect one specific water problem I could solve. Given the state of business following the Covid-19 lockdown, a fundamental problem business faced in learning and development was remote training. Fortunately, my experience included radio, video, and webinar development and delivery spanning more than twenty years.

MILE MARKER

Make sure you know what you do for your customers and ensure they know it too. Create clear messaging, so there is no confusion as to the problems you help customers solve.

MILE FORTY-FOUR – LEVERAGE YOUR SKILLS

Before selling cars, I took a part-time job as a board operator at KWVE radio in San Clemente, California. K-Wave was called "Southern California's Wave of Living Water." The station was owned and operated by Calvary Chapel of Costa Mesa. We played music, teaching programs, edited commercials (the old-fashioned way by splicing tape), and a few of us provided voices for the Saturday Morning Kids Show. My role included writing stories for the kid's show and hosting a brief daily sports report. It was short-lived because a listener called and complained directly to Pastor Chuck Smith that sports didn't belong on a Christian radio station. They'd been announcing Calvary Chapel High-School's wrestling and basketball scores for years during their news segments, which caused me to produce the broader sports report. Go figure.

There were opportunities to broadcast live events like The Harvest Crusades from both Anaheim Stadium and Jack Murphy Stadium in San Diego. These live broadcasts opened the door for me to host a weekend call-in talk show for KBRT Radio in Santa Ana, California called, "A Higher Perspective." And while my radio career didn't take off, the experience provided me skills useful for delivering virtual events and webinars.

Another opportunity in support of solving the "water problem" came during my first stint with Mitsubishi Motors. We were producing a series of sales training videos for the Mitsubishi Academy, but the budget didn't provide for high-level on-camera talent. Being raised in the home of an entertainer and having the opportunity to dance on live TV during an episode of the afternoon kid's show, "Engineer Bill's Shake Shop," I volunteered.

The first day on the set was an interesting one. The crew was not enthusiastic about me hosting. Ask any video production crew how they react when they hear the words, "the client is the talent," and you'll understand. But my experience with scripts and doing live radio gave me an edge. As it turned out, my video work is pretty decent. Reading a teleprompter effectively with few takes needed is one of my skills. They call it the ability to "rip and read" in the radio business.

There would eventually be a dozen or more sales training product and process videos for Mitsubishi, including the launch and training videos for Mitsubishi's first US version of the Lancer Evolution (EVO). Later I would learn to edit video and I wrote, produced, and directed a series for called "The Tip of the Day." I'm not sure if I came up with the idea for use in automotive learning or not, but it's certainly something being used with great success by several companies.

Today DelRae Learning and Development has contracts with three automotive clients and one client in the corporate culture space. We'd like to hire additional support staff with plans to grow the business into the premier source of online learning and development. In the meantime, one particular opportunity capitalizing on all the skills and experiences I've mentioned thus far has become an unexpected blessing and a highly sought-after series of events in the automotive industry called Ted Ings' Fixed Ops RoundTable.

MILE MARKER

Continue to develop skills and leverage the existing skills you have. When things change, you'll be able to bring your skills to bear in order and solve problems quickly and efficiently.

FORTY-SEVEN

MILE FORTY-FIVE - BE READY FOR OPEN DOORS

TED INGS HAS BEEN an on-off again business associate of mine since 2002. We've had great experiences together, and he also once canceled my contract. The timing of our separation was less than ideal for me. But as previously mentioned in stories regarding my experience with GM, it was a business decision not taken personally. If I had, there would have been no opportunity for my involvement in what has become an unexpected phenomenon in our industry called the Fixed Ops Roundtable.

Shortly before I left Mitsubishi in December 2019, Ted invited me to speak at an event in Los Angeles. It was the third in the Fixed Ops Roundtable series. The idea behind these events came from Mike Vogel, a personal friend of both Ted and mine. Neither of them could have expected the impact these events would have on the automotive industry. The event included about 100 total people. The following event (the day before NADA in Las Vegas) was double that, at over 200 people. Just this week, we had registrations for our Fixed Ops Roundtable Back to the Future event of over 500.

The event in Los Angeles was well received, but the meeting flow got a bit out of hand as speakers carried their message passed the allotted time. As a result of my flight schedule, I wasn't able to speak. Given the lack of control over the speakers, Ted asked Mike Vogel and I if we could help control the flow and timing of presenters at the next event in Las Vegas. We agreed. Ted also asked me to moderate a panel of guests related to new industry technologies, which I was happy to do. But what was supposed to be a simple act of escorting presenters on and off the stage based on an electronic clock turned into an opportunity for me to become the producer, director and facilitator of the Fixed Ops RoundTable virtual events.

It was February 14, 2020. Nobody had any idea the world was about to change due to Covid-19, nor that this would be the last live event anyone would be able to attend for quite some time. I arrived at the meeting room of the Embassy Suites Hotel in Las Vegas at about 6:30 a.m. The room was mostly set up, but one of the essential pieces of equipment had gone missing—the presenters' time clock. As a result, my new job became "5-Minute Warning Guy," making sure the presenters didn't overstay their speaking time.

As the day unfolded, my confidence and ability to gain eye contact with the speakers afforded us the ability to stay ahead of schedule all day long. My control over the event earned me a reputation as "The Hook." While Ted was worried that individual presenters would be challenging to manage, everyone graciously respected my direction.

Things went exceptionally well, and the reviews were exceptional. I earned the respect of many in attendance. How I moderated the panel and how all the participants stayed on time and task was a success.

MILE MARKER

When a door opens, walk through it, if only to see if there is an opportunity awaiting you. Be prepared mentally, physically, and professionally to enter in and perform at a high level with excellent results.

FORTY-EIGHT

MILE FORTY–SIX – GOOD RELATIONSHIPS EVENTUALLY PAY OFF

A FEW WEEKS after the event in Las Vegas, Ted called me and asked if I would speak at the next event scheduled for April 17, in Dallas, Texas. The Fixed Ops RoundTable Tire Summit would be the biggest and best of the roundtables yet. I agreed to participate, and I planned to introduce my automotive story alongside the FISH! Philosophy® at the event. Then Covid-19 hit. While most every other auto industry event was being canceled or postponed, Ted decided to take the event virtual. Some told him it was a mistake.

Ted contacted me and asked my opinion about the virtual event. He wanted to know if there were a company I could recommend for facilitation. Taking events like this virtual has been done many times before at the cost of between $30,000 to $50,000. At the time, we had no clue how much these companies charged, nor the amount of work involved behind the scenes to pull something like this off.

We've learned that we don't need to opt for a Learjet when a Cessna gets us to our destination. After I introduced Ted to a good friend whose company was more than capable of delivering a stellar product, Ted decided instead to ask me to facilitate the virtual meeting. Armed with my experience in radio, webinars, on-camera hosting, and a knowledge of the subject matter, I agreed. It also helped that I'd done video editing, directing, and project management.

The investment of time, study, practice, and preparation for an eight-hour event involving over forty presenters, commercials, teaser videos, and promotional activities is a huge undertaking. When recently asked by a podcast host what set me apart from others, I could only answer my online learning and training experience.

There are dozens of fantastic public speakers, trainers, facilitators, on-camera talent, producers, and directors, many of whom could do one or more of those things as good or better. I don't personally know anyone else in automotive who is capable of pulling off a virtual event like the Fixed Ops Roundtable on the budget we had at the level of quality and engagement Ted and I have been able to accomplish.

The fact that I can't name another person doesn't mean there isn't someone else who could pull it off, and it certainly isn't said out of pride or arrogance. Ted and I both knew we would need to follow up on our success with a product and result equal to or better than what we delivered in April 2020 if we were to continue to grow the event.

On June 18, 2020, we broadcast the Fixed Ops Roundtable – Back to the Future event that once again included over forty presenters to a constant audience of somewhere over 150 viewers for eight-plus hours. Over 500 participants registered, and there were 688 unique viewers during the event. The quality of speakers, production value, and content were much better. My friend John Traver said, "The last event was great, but this was 5X over the last one."

One thing we in the car business know is the concept of, "what have you done for me lately?" Retail automotive operates on a 30-day cycle of success or failure. We don't have much time to celebrate our position as top performers unless we deliver the same results month in and month out. Because of that, we didn't rest on success, and we aren't resting on the improved product either.

The day after the event, I sent a list of concerns to the broadcast provider to ensure an even better product next time. We learn more from each event, and both Ted and I want to make the product we produce something everyone can enjoy. We're upgrading our equipment, and we have regularly met with our platform provider to reduce the possibility of a system failure. We updated our processes and procedures for ourselves and our presenters, and we brought on new companies and new technologies to align with the "new normal" in automotive retail services. And still, there is more to improve.

Since my first day at Dave Swap Chevron, to my sales and fixed operations career at the Campbell Automotive Group and beyond, I have prepared for who I am and what I'm doing today. Along the way, my relationship with Jesus and my faith in God have helped mold me into the person I am and the businessman I am. As it is written, "Apart from me you can do nothing," Jesus said. The great news is it's written, "I can do all things through Christ who strengthens me."

MILE MARKER
Work hard to establish, build, and maintain excellent relationships. People are essential to you, and they need to know it. When times are tough, your relationships will carry the day.

FORTY-NINE

MILE FORTY–SEVEN – MAKE THE MOST OF SERENDIPITY

I'VE MET and established many great relationships through networking.

One of the benefits of my association with the Fixed Ops Roundtable has been building new business relationships and finding several great friends. One of those has developed into a mentor-to-mentor relationship with John Traver. I'd been familiar with John for twenty years because of his pioneering automotive BDCs. But until February of 2020, we'd never met. The fact that we met at all is ironic because the meeting took place in Las Vegas.

I don't like going to Las Vegas, and I would not have been there when John and I met were it not for the fact my daughter and two of our granddaughters moved there only a few months earlier. Yes, I was there for business. But at the time, I wasn't heavily involved in the Fixed Ops Roundtable, and I honestly would have skipped it were it not for my family being there. What an opportunity and a great friendship I would have missed. I would have also missed the chance to join John's company (Traver Companies) as the Director of Learning and Development. This is a role I just added to my portfolio during the final edits of this book. There are exciting times ahead!

Remember, we never arrive. The scripture says, "As iron sharpens iron, so one man (or woman) sharpens another." Coaches and mentors help us sharpen who we are by asking the right questions and offering ideas for us to consider. The opinions and insights of others are critical to personal development and professional growth. Suppose you don't have a mentor to seek one out. If you aren't mentoring others, make yourself available.

The real difference between a pond and a lake is flowing water. A pond becomes stagnant and can become deprived of oxygen over time, so nothing in it survives. By contrast, a lake has fresh water running into it from a river on one end, and out as the river continues on another end. The water in the lake is always turning over with new, fresh water. Lake water is fresher, cleaner, and has more life in it. Having a mentor and being a mentor makes you like a lake and not a pond.

MILE MARKER

Maximize unexpected opportunities and relationships. Know when a surprise of great value comes your way and don't waste it.

FIFTY

MILE FORTY-EIGHT – AFTER GOD, IT'S FAMILY FIRST

MY FAMILY IS important to me, and the feedback I receive most of the time is favorable. Occasionally, however, the feedback suggests my efforts toward my marriage and my family haven't been as positive as they should be. Has my family been a priority, or has it been mostly about me? It's an important question each of us should ask. Only you can answer the question for yourself.

You've seen how vital spiritual things are to me already. What may not be apparent is my belief that we can't possibly love God or be spiritual if we don't love others. Loving others is a clear teaching of Christ and many great philosophers.

Much of what we read on social media regarding success and achievement doesn't speak to the impact of personal success on the family. It's assumed that if our business makes good money and we provide enough things for our significant other and our kids, everyone will be happy. Not true. My most difficult times are when my choices have negatively impacted my wife and my family. For some, that doesn't matter because they value their success over their family or personal relationships.

Some suggest that we shouldn't let any criticism of our goals or dreams be allowed in our lives. It's a common thread in business books, motivational posts, and professional coaching. "Nobody should stop you from your dreams" is the clear message. They go so far as to suggest that if your family can't get on board, they must go away. That's not my opinion, though sometimes my behavior has appeared as if it were. There is still some work to be done.

We all have a decision to make. And we have to make tough choices daily. Some people do well not being married or not having a family. If you have a family, consider how much you prioritize them. Regularly ask yourself how they feel about the way you spend your time and how you prioritize their feelings.

MILE MARKER

If you have a family, put your family first. Don't be willing to risk losing your most important relationships over business success. Find a way to make sure your family's needs are met while still reaching your goals and dreams.

FIFTY-ONE

MILE FORTY–NINE – DON'T PLAY THE VICTIM

THERE HAVE BEEN plenty of opportunities to blame others when things went badly for me. I've done some work understanding myself and the impact my parents and others have had on why I do the things I do. But one thing I know to be a truth for everyone is we all have a choice regarding how we react to anything life brings our way. At any point in your life, you can freely choose your attitude.

In a recent interview with Brian Tracy, he told us many of the problems people face today is because they spend a lot of time dwelling on the past. I agree. The analogy I use most often is that of a scar. An accident at the age of 12 left me with thirty-two stitches on my lip and chin. There is a visible scar of about an inch in front of my face every morning when I shave. But it no longer hurts. It hasn't hurt for decades, even though the event's memory is right in front of my face every day. Most days, it goes unnoticed.

Hardly anyone asks me about my scar. The last time someone brought it up was at least ten years ago, and it made for a great story. Because my work has me on camera a lot, can you imagine what the impact would be if the scar were always on my mind? It's not. Ever!

Too often, people cherish the pain of past scars. They always dig at them, so the pain never goes away. As a result, they have an ongoing excuse for not being successful. Again, certain things like PTSD or chemical addiction are not addressed simply by choosing to forget them or choosing a different attitude. That's not the topic here. Most of us have the power to decide to let go of our negative feelings.

Sometimes we need the help of others to stand firm on our choices and make it through tough times. Yes, there are chemical, emotional, physical, and spiritual challenges that make it difficult to change our behaviors or lifestyles. But if you want to change, you can. If you want your life to be different, it can be. You must be willing to seek helpers, ask for help, and face the pain of change head-on.

MILE MARKER

Be a winner. Don't let the past defeat you. Get the help you need, and make sure you overcome every obstacle you face.

FIFTY-TWO

MILE FIFTY – THESE THINGS REMAIN

THE BIBLE IS COMPLICATED for many people. Living the principles in it doesn't have to be. Jesus made it simple when He said, "Love God with all your heart, mind, and strength, and love your neighbor as yourself." Do those two things, and you will fulfill everything required in scripture. The Apostle Paul later explained that after everything else, three things remained to guide our lives: Faith, hope, and love.

Believing in God, yourself, and others require faith in something or someone greater than yourself. If you look at the positives and have hope, you won't be disappointed because eventually, all things work out for our good. And finally, loving others will get you through the most challenging times life brings your way.

MILE MARKER

Love yourself and love others. Living a life of faith, hope, and love will lead to a lifetime of fruitfulness.

FIFTY-THREE

MILE FIFTY-ONE – STANDING UP FOR RIGHTEOUSNESS

WE WERE two weeks into the national tragedy that followed the death of George Floyd when my wife asked, "How do you feel about all this?" Our children had posted about it. Many of my associates changed their profile pictures or tag lines to show support. Some of my connections expressed outrage about others who called themselves leaders but continued to post content as if nothing had changed. Others remained silent.

Four of our five granddaughters would be categorized as mixed race. Two are African American, and two are Hispanic American. So, I certainly have feelings about the situation. The first time I saw the video of the officers' knee on George Floyd's neck, I asked out loud, "Why isn't anyone doing anything?" I told my wife nobody could honestly say what they would do until they are in the situation, but my emotions said, "At the risk of being arrested myself, I would have tackled that cop!" People captured it on video, but nobody came to George Floyd's rescue. I'm still not sure why and it's not fair to judge because I wasn't there to prove what I would or would not have done.

What I felt about the situation, and how I still think, is based on scripture and how we're told to behave. We are taught exactly how to treat other people. Both the Old and New Testaments teach us how to treat foreigners, strangers, the poor and needy, widows and orphans, government officials, and more. It always shows respect, dignity, and kindness, with a few exceptions.

I've heard people bash scripture and the God of the Bible because of specific commands mostly found in the Old Testament. Aside from war, physical violence or punishment against others was only condoned outside the nation of Israel due to idol worship (which was accompanied by abhorrent behaviors such as self-mutilation, bestiality, and child sacrifice), or within their national laws to promote civil order. Violence was never condoned for the sake of emotional retribution.

How I felt, then, was angry and remorseful. My heart and attitude are the same toward all people regardless of race, religion, creed, gender, or political position. Everyone and anyone can behave well or badly. I support behaviors that are based on faith, hope, and love. I support justice. God will have the final say in all of it.

In my opinion, the most shameful acts in the aftermath of this tragedy are the behavior of politicians, so-called ministers, media, protesters, athletes, corporations, and individuals who have taken a tragic situation like the death of George Floyd and turned it into an opportunity to promote their agendas and world views. Many could care less about George Floyd, his family, the Black community, or the police and their families. They certainly don't care about the people of our nation or the world as a whole.

Changes are needed. I too have much to learn. In my opinion, the solution was written in stone by the hand of God thousands of years ago, and Jesus himself clarified the application in a mountain sermon and other times during his ministry. Jesus never marched against the Roman government, nor did he incite protests against a specific people group (which is one of the reasons he was rejected as Messiah).

The only property he destroyed was in the temple that he called both his Father's house and in how he compared it to his own body. In other words, he destroyed the property he owned. In that sense, "We the People" are the government, and the property belongs to the taxpayers. Then, there may be justification to show contempt for a system that promotes injustice by taking action against buildings and monuments, but only according to Constitutional law. And we don't own the property of private citizens and business owners.

Do you want solutions? Do you want to effect change? Read and live according to God's word, and it will happen for you. You can't change someone else.

Culturally, historically, and because of our society, it will be challenging to make this happen, but here are three scriptures to consider when understanding the Christian worldview:

Acts 4:14 – "There was not a needy person among them, for as many as were owners of lands or houses sold them and brought the proceeds of what was sold and laid it at the apostle's feet, and it was distributed to each as any had need."

(NOTE: This was a freewill choice of the believing

community, not a government program. And everyone was expected to work within the community except for the sick and invalid. It is, and always has been, the church's responsibility to meet the needs of their flock. If the Body of Christ behaved as we should, welfare would be all but eliminated in this country. That is on us, and it is on me.)

Mark 10:45 – "For even the Son of Man came not to be served but to serve, and to give his life as a ransom for many." What a powerful attitude and mindset. The Creator of the universe (He created all things, and all things belong to Him) chose service as the model for leadership, rather than sitting on a throne he rightfully deserved.

Finally, Malachi 3:5 addresses problems on both sides of the political aisle, and the main problem we all have. It says, "So, I (God) will come to put you on trial. I will be quick to testify against sorcerers, adulterers, and perjurers..."

The above is the part of the verse conservatives love to quote, but it continues,

"...against those who defraud laborers of their wages, who oppress the widows and the fatherless, and deprive the foreigners among you of justice..."

That is the part liberals love to quote. And the passage ends with,

"...but do not fear me," says the Lord Almighty.

None of the politicians like to quote the last part of the verse because their behavior would be based on the fear (awe) of God. Unfortunately, it isn't.

It's important to understand we can't choose what verses of the Bible to quote to justify our position. We must take the whole. In this case, both sides are right, and both sides are wrong.

My solution? "Seek first the kingdom of God and His

righteousness, and all these things will be added to you." – Matthew 6:33

MILE MARKER

Stand up for the rights of all people. Be willing to put your life on the line to stand up for what is right, because if you don't, you may lose your freedom.

FIFTY-FOUR

MILE FIFTY-TWO – LOOSEN UP

AFTER THE PREVIOUS LESSON, this may appear to be a polar opposite. That's the beauty of life. There are many characteristics of our journey. Life is tough enough without taking it seriously all the time. Laughing, dancing, playing, singing, and other fun activities are essential for mental health and successful living. A proverb says, "A glad heart makes a cheerful face, but by sorrow of heart, the spirit is crushed." Look on the bright side!

It's essential to take care of yourself by planning time in your days, weeks, and months to enjoy "the fruits of your labor." Take vacations. Take care of your body. Eat good food and enjoy your family and friends.

In the FISH! Philosophy® the principles of Play and Make Their Day serve as a reminder to make life meaningful. Get outside the board room, the spreadsheets, and the call-center and have some fun. Life is too short. Don't make it only about business.

MILE MARKER

Don't take life too seriously. Work hard and apply wisdom. Understand there are things beyond your control. Keep a light touch on the world and embrace what matters most.

FIFTY-FIVE

JUST A REST STOP

THIS BOOK IS one of two I planned to publish in 2020, but both were published in 2021. The purpose of each is different. My intention here was to give the reader some ideas and perspectives from things in my professional career that can help them learn and grow. In so doing, maybe you can achieve the success you didn't believe was possible before you read The Miles and the Markers.

Another reason for writing this book was to establish credibility. People outside my network don't have a clue about me or my accomplishments. One person associated with the Fixed Ops Roundtable introduced me to their CEO as "Ted's sidekick." Anyone viewing me like a sidekick doesn't have a clue about my experience or my level of qualifications. But that's not their fault.

My next book is a novel. It's a story about a boy running from his past and toward a future he wants to make. It's not a biography. It's entirely fictitious. But you will find some of me in the main character and other characters. There are lessons to be sure, some of which cross over from this book, but none that will look familiar on the surface.

I've also begun a new relationship with John Traver and his businesses. In addition to operating DelRae Learning and Development (now as a side hustle), I'm excited to be taking on the role of Director of Learning and Development for Traver Companies.

Finally, it's a beginning. I hope to write a book with my wife and other writings because there are many stories to tell. I'm so thankful to my friends, connections, family, and especially my wife for the support and encouragement they give me. Thank you for reading.

ACKNOWLEDGMENTS

So many people deserve to be mentioned for helping me achieve what I have so far. Many already have been mentioned. Because I don't want to miss anyone I haven't already named, I'll acknowledge people by the companies and groups who helped me with my career. This includes, but isn't limited to:

- My coaches at Bothell High School
- The brothers and sisters at Calvary Fellowship – Seattle, Calvary Northshore, and Ocean Hills Community Church
- The teachers and administrators at Capistrano Valley Christian Schools
- Those who worked at KWVE and KBRT Radio
- The team members at Saturn and Saab of Orange County
- Authors, teachers and mentors like Jim Rohn, Zig Ziglar, Brian Tracy, Jim Cathcart, and Bobb Biehl

- Saturn's Retail Training Team and all of their vendor partners
- The team at The Mitsubishi Academy, CX Department, field team members, and administrative support folks at Mitsubishi Motors North America
- The team and trainers from Auto University, and those involved with the project for Mazda North American Operations
- Southwest Airlines
- My friends and business associates on LinkedIn and The Fixed Ops Roundtable®
- The team at Charthouse Learning

There are also a few special family friends like the Phil Jones Family, and John and Patty Payne. And there are others.

Of most importance is my family. I wouldn't be where I am today without the love and support of my parents, siblings, and in-laws. I am blessed to have four wonderful children who have blessed us with five amazing granddaughters.

Finally, there's Patty. She is, "The love of my youth. My Patty Rae." Without you babe, none of this would have mattered. You are the one person in the world who really knows who I am, and still, you love me. I'm excited about our future and the legacy we get to leave before we meet our Savior. I love you.

I am a man, born from above. I worship and serve Jesus as Lord and Christ. I see all people as imagers of God, and capable of providing light and love, grace and mercy, kindness and compassion to others.

May your miles be traveled in peace, health, and safety. And may the markers you see along the way bring you wisdom and insight for your journey.

THOUGHTS FROM TRAVELERS

"Gene opens his heart and shares some wonderful stories about his life. And in doing so gives us 52 life lessons on how the choices we make shape our lives. Go and shape yours intentionally."
    John Christensen
    Creator of The Fish! Philosophy®
    Co-Author of FISH!

"Life journeys. No two are the same. Gene's remarkable life journey is filled with depth and wisdom!"
    John Traver
    CEO Traver Companies

"From HOF pitcher, Don Sutton, to service station days with Dave Swap and lessons from The Carpenter...Every Mile Marker delivers very personal, relatable and authentic life lessons. I can completely identify with so much of the book, because of its intimacy. One particular lesson that stood out for me was when Gene "accepted" the offer to ride along to Tehachapi State Prison. I can appreciate the serendipitous nature of the story, as he grudgingly accompanies his mother anticipating a long, boring ride, only to be counseled by the great Don Sutton on the art and philosophy behind the hitter's worst nightmare, a perfectly timed and executed deuce! Flip the pages and enjoy the ride!"
    Sandi P Cerami
    Speaking Professional & Consultant

"The miles and the mile markers... I love that title! To me, it means that it's about the experience, and our experience, and the learning along the way that makes our journey so meaningful.

Gene Girdley weaves a wonderful narrative of his life and the lessons he's learned along the way. As usual, he brings his stories to life in a wonderfully engaging way. If you've ever been lucky enough to see Gene in a classroom, or just had the pleasure of sharing a cup of coffee with him, you know what I'm talking about...

Buckle your seatbelt's and get ready for a fun ride! Thanks so much Gene for sharing your story with us, and the incredible lessons that resonate within us all."

Joseph Jordan
Performance Coach
Momentum Performance Improvement

Made in the USA
Middletown, DE
06 March 2021